A
PREFACE TO
LOGIC

BY

Morris R. Cohen

DOVER PUBLICATIONS, INC.

NEW YORK

Published in Canada by General Publishing Com-
pany, Ltd., 30 Lesmill Road, Don Mills, Toronto,
Ontario.
Published in the United Kingdom by Constable
and Company, Ltd., 10 Orange Street, London
WC2H 7EG.

This Dover edition, first published in 1977, is an
unabridged, unaltered republication of the work
originally published by Henry Holt and Company,
Inc., New York, in 1944.

International Standard Book Number: 0-486-23517-3
Library of Congress Catalog Card Number: 77-075235

Manufactured in the United States of America
Dover Publications, Inc.
180 Varick Street
New York, N.Y. 10014

To the College of the City of New York
and its students who gave zest to my life
this volume is dedicated

Contents

Foreword

In the history of ideas the past century is one marked by an extraordinary development of logic. A discipline which had remained for more than 20 centuries in approximately the state to which the mind of Aristotle reduced it, suddenly entered upon a period of rapid growth and systematic development. While the essential elements of the Aristotelian logic have not been overthrown or shaken, the labors of Boole, Peirce, Schröder, Frege, Russell, Whitehead, and a host of fellow workers have produced a calculus of classes and a calculus of propositions in which the Aristotelian theory of the syllogism is seen to occupy only a tiny corner. The potentialities of the new logic as a scientific instrument have already been indicated in the illumination which the application of modern logic has brought to the foundations of mathematics. There is reason to hope that parallel results may soon be achieved in other fields.

Unfortunately, however, periods of rapid and extensive development of a science are frequently periods of loose thinking about the foundations of the science itself. Such was the case with mathematics in the eighteenth century and with biology in the nineteenth. So it is today that the philosophic significance of the new logic, the character of its presuppositions, and the directions of its possible application are problems which have attracted relatively little reflective thought. Indeed, with a sort of perverse professional modesty, many of our most brilliant contemporary logicians have insisted that the subject of their study is simply marks on paper, or symbols generally, without relevance to the objective realities that are explored by the natural and social sciences.

It may be that this attitude represents a healthy reaction away from the excessive claims of an absolutistic rationalism that sought to derive answers to all questions from pure reason without recognizing that reason can produce material conclusions only if it starts with material premises. It is only natural that the excesses of Kantian and Hegelian absolutism should have produced an extreme reaction the essence of which is the denial of objective reality to reason and logic. But the truth is not to be found at either extreme in these swings of the intellectual pendulum. A world of isolated atomic facts without interrelationship would be as completely unintelligible as a world of logical relations which did not relate anything to anything else. Reflection shows that logic cannot be isolated from any realm of being, cannot, for example, be confined to the analysis or description of thought or of symbolism, even assuming it were possible to have thought without objects, or symbols without things symbolized. Indeed, logic could not possibly illumine thoughts and symbols if it did not illumine that which is the object of thought and symbolism. If logic were indeed only a manipulation of symbols it would be as devoid of philosophical significance and scientific utility as chess or tick-tack-toe.

To put the matter affirmatively we may say that formal logic is the heart of philosophy precisely because the subject matter of logic is the formal aspect of all being, an aspect not only of objects and events in time and space but equally of nonspatial and nontemporal relations of objects. The relation of incompatibility is as hard an objective fact as the relations of subtraction, intersection, gravitation, digestion, warfare, or any of the other relations that form the subject matter of science. From this standpoint it becomes possible and important to explore the relations of logic to such fields of study as natural science, ethics, history, and general philosophy. Such an exploration is the motif that runs through this work.

This volume does not purport to be a treatise on logic. Whatever slight contributions I have been able to make to the substance of logical doctrine have been made elsewhere. What is attempted in the studies that form this volume is an exploration of the periphery of logic, the relations of logic to the rest of the universe, the philosophical presuppositions which give logic its meaning, and the applications which give it importance. If this voyage of exploration does not settle any of the domains surveyed, I trust that it may at least dispel some doubts as to the existence of these domains and perhaps persuade some who are now inclined to waiver that here are fertile fields which will richly repay honest intellectual labor.

Implicit in these essays is a view of logic which, although amply justified, I think, by modern technical developments, may appear somewhat shocking to readers brought up on the traditional logic of the older textbooks. Thus the field of logic has been traditionally restricted to propositions true or false in themselves; the realm of fiction and fictions has appeared to lie beyond the ken of logic. But development of the concepts of system and order in the newer logic show this limitation to be unjustified. Sentences which have a variable truth value relative to a defining set of postulates or hypotheses are as susceptible to logical analysis as any of the sentences about the mortality of Socrates that filled the older textbooks. Again, the traditional logic has seemed to assume a world of hard and fast concepts, a world in which everything is black or white and where there are no gradations or twilight zones. But modern logic is a more flexible instrument than the Aristotelian syllogism, and it is fully capable of dealing with the world of probabilities and uncertainties which is the true object of science and the material of daily life.

Conceived in these terms, logic becomes not a restriction upon the world that science discloses but an indispensable instrument for the exploration of possibilities, and in this sense an indispensable element of liberal civilization and free thought. That such a view of logic can help to dispel some of the mists which envelop contemporary philosophizing is the faith in which these fragmentary studies are presented.

M. R. C.

A PREFACE TO LOGIC

I

The Subject Matter of Formal Logic [1]

1. *The Subject Matter of Books on Logic*

If by logic is meant a clear, accurate, and orderly intellectual procedure, then the subject of logic, as presented in current text-books, comes near being the most illogical in our chaotic curriculum. Defined almost universally as dealing with the laws of thought and devoting considerable space to the way in which the mind proceeds or fails to proceed in conception, judgment, and reasoning, it is neither clearly distinguished from psychology nor frankly treated as a branch of that modern universal science.

In addition, the following miscellany is interjected into our science, designed to train young people in the habits of clear thinking: (1) Linguistic information as to the meaning and use of words, extending often to their history, and grammatical considerations as to the structure of sentences; (2) rhetorical considerations as to the persuasive force of various arguments; (3) metaphysical considerations as to the reality or unreality of universals and particulars and their relations; (4) epistemologic, i.e., mixed psychologic and metaphysical, considerations as to the nature of knowledge and its relation to what is called the world of reality; (5) catalogues of miscellaneous ancient errors, under the head of material fallacies; (6) pedagogic directions as to the conduct of the human understanding, teaching us how to

[1] The substance of this chapter was read before the American Philosophical Association, December, 1917, and published in *The Journal of Philosophy*, vol. 15 (1918), p. 673.

discover the cause of typhoid or of some other disease of which the cause is already known; (7) miscellaneous general considerations of various other sciences and their histories, which pretend to describe the essence of scientific method; and (8) the rudiments of formal or symbolic logic, as in the theory of classes or syllogisms, which, as developed in such books as Couturat's *Algebra of Logic,* is strictly a mathematical science, though it need not necessarily be expressed in special symbols.

Mixed studies, like mixed races and mixed constitutions, show the greatest vitality, and there could be no valid objection to the same textbook treating all these important matters, provided the information given were accurate and the various points of view clearly distinguished. As to the accuracy of the information, especially in the sections on scientific method, my respect for distinguished professional colleagues compels silence, but I may say that a blameless life as a minister of the gospel or as a college teacher does not qualify one, even after he has consulted previous textbooks on logic, to become an authority on the methods of the various sciences—topics which can be dealt with justly only by the masters of such sciences. My main point, however, is that the failure clearly to distinguish between the various points of view just mentioned has bred a great deal of the confusion of modern philosophy. I am not certain that logic can do much to train students in the habits of clear thinking. But logic ought certainly not to infect eager and trustful young minds with fundamental confusions, confusions which determine the setting of subsequent philosophizing. If this negative precept seem unimportant, it is well to remember that modern hospital methods were revolutionized by Florence Nightingale, I believe, by this very insistence that, whatever else hospitals may do, they should not spread disease.

2. *Logic as the Science of Thought*

Nearly all the books define logic as in some manner the science of thought. But that the laws of logic are not the universal laws according to which we do actually think is conclusively shown, not only by the most elementary observation or introspection, but by the very existence of fallacies. Nor do we free ourselves completely from this difficulty by saying that logic deals with the laws according to which we think when we think correctly. Assuredly, correct thinking takes place only under favorable physiological, educational, and moral conditions. But we do not expect any treatise on logic to deal with the physiologic and moral conditions of mental health. To define logic as dealing with the laws according to which we ought to think does not define its distinctive subject, since the principles of every science are in a sense laws according to which we ought to think if we would think correctly on its distinctive subject matter.

3. *Formal and Material Truths*

The distinctive subject matter of logic, constituting, as a matter of fact, the core of the traditional Aristotelian logic, is what is called formal truth. The distinction between material and formal truth, like the related distinction between assumption and proof or between immediate and mediate truth, is not without its difficulties. But it is clear that we must distinguish between the factual truth of any proposition and the truth of the assertion that it logically follows from, or necessitates as consequences, certain other propositions. It is one thing to assert categorically that Nineveh fell in 622 B.C. and quite another to assert that, if it did, it must have preceded and cannot have followed the Scythian invasion of 621 B.C. It is one thing to assert that through a point outside a straight line only one parallel can be drawn, but quite another matter to assert that, whether that proposition is true or not, from it and certain other propositions it necessarily follows that the sum of the angles of a triangle is equal to two right angles.

In any given context it is relatively easy to distinguish between the categoric assertion that a given proposition is true and the formal truth, validity, correctness or adequacy of the proof or demonstration that it follows from certain other propositions. In any given case, also, it is rather easy to see that the material truth of premises or conclusion and the validity of the proof may be relatively independent of each other—a proposition known to be false may be correctly proved (from false premises), and the proof of a true proposition may be formally defective. But when we come to deal with the general nature of formal truth and its relation to material truth we begin to encounter difficulties. Many, however, of the traditional difficulties may be eliminated if we take the trouble to distinguish clearly between reasoning or inference as an operation or event which happens in an individual mind and the question of evidence or general conditions under which what is asserted can be true. When this is recognized it becomes clear that logical or formal truths are truths concerning the implication, consistency, or necessary connection between *objects* asserted in propositions, and the distinctive subject matter of logic may be said to be the relations generally expressed by *if—then necessarily.*

Terms and relations, matter and form, immediate and mediate truth, are like north and south poles, strict correlatives, clearly distinguishable and inseparable—the existence of each is necessary to give meaning to the other. But obsessed by the monistic prejudice, philosophers have refused to recognize any ultimate polarity or duality,[2] and have perpetually sought to reduce everything either to form or to content. The former effort leads to empty panlogism, the latter to dumb mysticism. Without pretending to settle the problem we may avoid the dilemma by recognizing that matter and form are strictly correlatives in every concrete situation, and that when we take the world of science as a whole it is found to contain besides logical relations an alogical element which no efforts of panlogism have successfully eliminated. At any rate there is no insuperable objection to the

---

[2] This difficulty of philosophers is precisely that of the exuberant individual who puzzled two policemen with the problem, "Which side of the street is the other side?"

assertion that logical truth or consistency is a genuine part of the world of truth which science studies.

What we call the evidence for the material or factual truth of any proposition involves—excepting matters of immediate apprehension which are beyond argument—the question of the logical relation between the proposition in question and certain others which are taken for granted. Thus, we rule out the proposition that there is life on the planet Mercury, by the proposition that life cannot exist except at certain temperatures, etc. In the same way the question of formal truth enters as an integral part of the material truth of what have been called practical propositions. Thus all of the practical judgments recently called to the attention of logicians by Professor Dewey can be put in the traditional hypothetical form of formal logic—if you want to recover, you must see a doctor, etc.[3] Indeed the relation of means to end is logically only one type of the relation of parts to wholes. This can readily be seen when we compare with the foregoing practical judgments such theoretic judgments as, to complete the square you must add one to both members of the equation, or to reduce nine to seven subtract two, etc.

Similarly, formal consistency forms part of artistic or dramatic truth. If Hamlet is a prince, he must act consistently with the supposed nobility of that character. If he has studied many years at Wittenberg, he must show the scholar's aptitude for reflection on both sides of the question, to be or not to be.

It may be objected that in all these latter examples we are dealing with matters of fact that are contingent and not at all logically necessary. Life on this planet has been empirically found to exist between certain temperatures. In other planets it might be different. Even on this planet people may get well without consulting a doctor, princes may be undignified, and those who study at Wittenberg may not reflect at all. This objection, however, in no way militates against our account of the nature of the logical or formal relation. The objector raises an

[3] It is because in practical judgments, the protasis or conditional clause is understood and not expressed that there arises the seeming difference.

issue of fact. He challenges the material truth of the major premises assumed in these examples and not the necessity of the inferences drawn from them. This raises in each case an issue of fact to be settled by evidence, but it leaves unaffected the logical test of necessity which is, whether it is or is not possible for the antecedent to be true and the consequent to be false at the same time. In a world in which all princes are dignified it is impossible for Hamlet to act like a clown; and if the Hamlet on the stage does behave like a clown he only irritates us by his failure to live in the world of our assumption. When we demonstrate or prove a proposition in physics, e.g., that if there were two bodies the smaller would on receiving a tangential motion describe an ellipse about the larger, we show that it is impossible for certain accepted principles (the law of gravitation) to be true and the demonstrated proposition to be false. When we come to the demonstrations of pure mathematics we do not restrict our postulate to any particular universe, but are concerned with the universe of all possible meaning. $2 + 2 = 5$ is impossible, in any universe in which 2, 5, and $=$ have the meanings assigned in our arithmetic.

4. *The Distinction Between the Formal and the Meaningless*

The need for considering the formal implications of an hypothesis, independently of the question whether it is in fact true, has led to the erroneous view that formal logic considers the consequences of propositions apart from their meaning. It ought to be clear, however, that a proposition devoid of all meaning would be just nonsense from which nothing could possibly be deduced. The particular logical consequences of any proposition surely do not follow from the mere sounds or marks on paper but from the nature of the facts asserted in the proposition. All scientific procedure, however, rests upon our ability to consider the abstract general characteristics possessed by all the objects of a group, leaving out of account the more specific nature in which they differ. Thus mechanics considers the mass and motion of bodies apart from their color, relative scarcity, or other property; and even more specialized sciences like crystallography, bio-chemistry or genetics, all consider isolated or abstract properties possessed by widely different objects. Similarly it is possible for logic to abstract from the specific concrete meaning of propositions those elements which are common to whole classes of propositions, and to denote these common elements by suitable symbols. When, therefore, mathematical logicians use such forms as *p implies q*, they are not talking about propositions devoid of all meaning but about a certain property of classes of propositions.

The term property has a somewhat misleading connotation. It suggests an inert quality inhering in a substance. It may, therefore, be advisable to substitute the notion of operation or transformation for that of property.

In social usage, formal rules are rules of procedure applicable to all the members of a given class, irrespective of any personal characteristics such members may have. In the same way, every science has its rule of operation or laws according to which all the objects it studies can be combined. Logic is the most general of all the sciences; it deals with the elements or operations common to all of them. That is, rules of logic are the rules of operation or transformation according to which all possible objects, physical, psychical, neutral, or complexes can be combined. Thus, logic is an exploration of the field of most general abstract possibility. This may make logical information very thin; but it is not therefore devoid of significance. Not only does it rule out impossibilities but it reveals the possibilities of hypotheses other than those usually taken for granted; and in this respect it frees the mind and contributes not only to the fixed form but to the living growth of science. The history of science shows beyond doubt that the vital factor in the growth of any science is not the Baconian passive observation but the active questioning of nature, which is furthered by the multiplication of hypotheses as hypotheses.

5. *The Use of Logical Symbols*

The foregoing explanation of what we mean by formal rules explains the great utility of symbols not only in logic and mathematics but in all exact sciences.

Whatever be the psychologic nature of the reasoning process, it is a fact that this process is facilitated by the use of artificial counters or symbols which represent only the general properties under investigation and not any of the specific properties which must be excluded. As the rules according to which our symbols can be combined are by hypothesis precisely those according to which the entities they denote can be combined, it follows that it is not necessary that we keep the concrete meaning or cash value of our counters always before us. If our reasoning is correct the meaning of our final result follows from our initial assumptions; and this, I take it, is one of the great advantages of any calculus or system of symbolic manipulation.

The employment of special symbols instead of the more familiar symbols called words, is a practical convenience rather than a logical necessity. There is not a proposition in logic or mathematics that cannot be ultimately expressed in ordinary words (this is proved by the fact that these subjects can be taught to those who do not start with a knowledge of the special symbols). But practically it is impossible to make much progress in mathematics and logic without appropriate symbols, just as it is impossible to carry on modern trade without checks or book credits, or to build modern bridges without special tools. Symbolic reasoning is essentially reasoning on a large scale with instruments appropriate to such wholesale undertakings. If we want a large number of fish, we must use nets rather than single lines. The opposition to symbolic reasoning, like the old opposition to the introduction of machinery, arises from the natural disinclination to change, to incur trouble or expense for a future gain. The prejudice against careful analytic procedure is part of the human impatience with technique which arises from the fact that men are interested in results and would like to attain them without the painful toil which is the essence of our mortal finitude.

6. *Logic and Mathematics*

The nature of the subject matter of logic may be better understood when it is seen to be identical with the subject matter of pure mathematics. This identity of logic and pure mathematics is the discovery of the nineteenth century, and was not possible before the discovery of non-Euclidean geometry and of multiple algebra revealed the true nature of pure mathematics. From the days of Plato to those of Kant, geometry was viewed exclusively as a science of physical space, and as the Euclidean axioms were regarded as self-evidently true, it was possible for Kant and his predecessors to maintain the existence of an *a priori* knowledge of nature. The discovery of non-Euclidean geometry shows that the axioms of the traditional geometry are convenient assumptions and not *a priori* necessities of thought or perception. Their contraries have been proved capable of receiving an equivalent logical and mathematical development, so that pure geometry alone is incapable of deciding the question of whether physical space is Euclidean or not. Geometry, as a branch of pure mathematics, serves only to develop the necessary consequences of various hypotheses or assumptions.

Similar considerations apply to algebra, which used to be defined as the general science of number or quantity. The discovery of the real nature of the so-called imaginary numbers, and the consequent development of the various types of complex numbers and of various types of algebra, have brought out clearly that all algebra is essentially a calculus of the implication of certain rules of operation or combination. The commutative and associative laws of addition and multiplication are not necessities of thought, but assumptions which define specific transformations applicable only to those fields of nature to which they are empirically found to be applicable. But the rules or postulates of any algebra being laid down, the development is a matter of pure logic. Algebraic proofs are in every respect logical proofs and depend no more on any special element of intuition than does logic itself.

The old notion that mathematics is restricted to quantity has been discarded as erroneous; there are branches of mathematics, such as analysis situs, in which quantities do not enter at all. What is essential to mathematics is that, given a set of premises, the conclusion will follow in all cases. For pedagogic or administrative purposes it may still be necessary to refrain from identifying mathematics with the whole region of necessary inferences in which all exact science is located, but in point of fact there is no strictly logical difference between pure mathematics and deductive reasoning. What we usually call formal logic is simply the study of the most general portion of pure mathematics.

The assertion of the identity of logic and pure mathematics has appeared as a paradox and as a stone of stumbling to many philosophers, and even to some mathematicians. Surely, they tell us, a proposition about circles, quintic equations or prime numbers belongs to a different science than a proposition about syllogisms. This objection is perfectly valid so long as we uncritically accept the views of mathematics and logic of our traditional school textbooks. If, e.g., circles are viewed as objects in space, like stones or caterpillars, while logic deals with "laws of thought as such," then all talk about the identity of logic and geometry is sheer intellectual violence. But to take this view is to ignore the distinction between pure and applied mathematics. If we view circles as existing things in actual or physical space, then geometry is a branch of physics or applied mathematics—the simplest branch of mechanics, as Newton has indicated in the preface to the *Principia*. But geometry as a branch of pure mathematics is in no way concerned with the existence of circles in the physical world. Euclidean and non-Euclidean hypotheses cannot simultaneously be true of the physical world if their terms denote the same entities, yet they are all equally legitimate branches of pure geometry, as is also the geometry of a four-dimensional space.

Geometry, as a branch of pure mathematics, is interested in a problem of logical proof: whether if certain propositions (axioms, etc.) are true, certain other propositions must be so likewise. In the construction of its chain of demonstration, geometry, as has been shown by Pieri, Hilbert and others, does not need to use any concept except those definable in terms of the fundamental notions of logic (classes, relations, etc.), nor does it need to assume any primitive proposition except those assumed in logic. In pure geometry, then, propositions about points and lines are replaced by propositions about classes of indefinables and relations between them. You may object on linguistic grounds, that propositions about classes and relations ought not to be called geometry, and that unless we continue to identify the indefinable "points" with the intuitable spots on paper or blackboard, we ought not to keep the name geometry; but the significant fact remains that if you examine any rigorous treatise on plane geometry, you will find that it will make no difference in the form and sequence of our propositions if our indefinable points are replaced by complex numbers, or if "distance between points" is replaced by differences of holiness in a multi-dimensional series of saints.

7. *Deduction and Novelty*

A serious obstacle to the recognition of the identity of the subject matter of logic and that of pure mathematics, an obstacle that has had a great influence on philosophers and mathematicians like Poincaré, is the assumption of the ancient dogma that in strict deduction there can be nothing in the conclusion which is not already contained in the premises. From this it is argued that mathematics, so fertile in unexpected discoveries, cannot be purely deductive. Any argument that a certain thing cannot be is refuted if we can actually show it, and to the contention that mathematics cannot be reduced to formal logic, the actual doing of it by Frege, Peano, Pieri, and Whitehead and Russell is sufficient refutation. It is instructive, however, to examine the dogma at the basis of this obstinate refusal to admit an established fact, especially since the dogma is closely related to the generally accepted but essentially obscure dictum that all knowledge comes from experience.

The notion that deductive reasoning must necessarily be a sterile series of tautologies arises from the failure to distinguish between psychologic, physical, and logical considerations. Psychologically it is obviously not true that the conclusion is always contained in the premises. For ages men accepted the elementary laws of arithmetic without seeing that they involve as a necessary consequence the proposition that there are no two numbers whose ratio is the square root of two. Or, to take a more concrete example, I may know that the *Camperdown* was sunk and none aboard could be saved, and I may know also that Smith sailed aboard that ill-fated vessel. And yet it may be some time before the union of these two propositions flashes on my mind the startling conclusion that Smith must have been drowned.[4] To suppose that when we think of any proposition or group of propositions, we always have in mind all their logical consequences is a supposal inconsistent with the fact that many find the study of mathematics difficult or are easily tripped by lawyers on cross-examination. Nor is strict deduction incompatible with the existence of physical novelty, i.e., with the coming into being at certain moments of time of that which did not exist at previous moments of time. The fact that the moon is every moment in a new position does not make it impossible to deduce a comprehensive formula for its path out of a few past observations and the hypothesis of universal gravity.

The consequences in a deductive system, then, may be new

[4] The silly character of the old argument that every syllogism involves a *petitio principi* because no universal can be known before we know all the particulars under it, becomes clear when we take a practical syllogism such as, all persons convicted of crime should be disfranchised, my brother has been convicted, etc. Jephthah said, Whoever cometh forth, etc. Yet he was surprised when his daughter proved to be the one.

in time as well as psychologically startling or unexpected, and yet there will be no proposition in our series which is not necessitated by the premises. The difficulty with the traditional doctrine arises from the prevailing confusion between the process of thinking or learning which takes place in time, and the logical relations discovered, which do not form a temporal series at all. *In natura rerum* premises do not exist prior to their conclusion any more than they exist to the right or to the left of them. The spatial and temporal order is of very wide application, but we must guard against its undue extension. Thus it is well to note that when we speak of the conclusion being contained in the premises, we are resorting to an uncritical spatial metaphor. The inexhaustible theorems of algebra are assuredly not contained in its few axioms or primitive propositions in the way in which the chairs and other objects are contained in a room. All the possible games of chess that can be played can be deduced from the few rules of that game. But the games are not literally contained in these rules. The notion of containing may, indeed, be used in a wider sense to denote a certain relation of order, of which the spatial relation of container and contained is one instance. But in this wider sense not only are the games contained in the rules but the rules are contained in the multitude of games, as invariant changes or transformations common to all of them. The particular is in one sense part of the universal but in another sense the universal is simply that part or aspect of the particular which is the object of study.

The tremendous usefulness of general propositions and the predilection of Greek rationalism and medieval authoritarianism have spread the view that general truths have something of a superior status, superior certainty, superior authority and what not. But in respect of logic, premises and conclusions are on the democratic basis of strict correlatives. Logic shows that certain premises are sufficient or necessary for certain conclusions or that certain conclusions necessarily follow from certain premises. *The categoric assertion of either premises or conclusions involves something more than logic.* If, then, the laws of logic are rules of combination, nothing can be deduced from them except various combinations of logical rules. And it is as impossible to derive physical or psychologic truth from pure logic as to build a house with nothing except the rules of architecture. To say, however, that there is nothing in any logically or mathematically developed science except what is contained in its data is to say that there is nothing in a building except what is contained in its bricks, mortar, and other materials. The form or structure of a house is constituted by the system of relations between the material entities which make it up; and the form or structure which logic studies is the system of relations which hold between all possible objects that can be ordered into a system.

8. *Logic and the Nature of Mind*

According to the prevailing view, the relations between premises and conclusion exist in the mind only. This means either that terms and propositions apart from their relations exist in the so-called external world, or else that nothing at all exists outside of the mind. If we put terms in one world and relations in another, it is difficult to see how the terms can have an intelligible or knowable character, and how relations in one universe can be said to be the relations of terms in another. This is the basis of the familiar but unanswerable difficulties of epistemology—how ideas in a mind can know things in a world external to it. If, on the other hand, the terms logically related also exist in the mind, then the distinction between logic and physics is still to be maintained, and the distinction between the two cannot be derived from their common mental nature. One engaged in an actual logical or mathematical investigation can no more make any special progress towards a definite solution of a problem by invoking any doctrine as to the nature of mind or thought than he can by invoking a theory as to the nature of God and His providence.

9. *Logical Necessity and Contingency*

It has always been recognized that logic deals with relations that are necessary, but the nature of necessary relations has been obscured, first, by the Stoic confusion between that which is necessary and that which is generally accepted, and by the modern identification of necessity with psychologic certainty. Obviously, the existence of fallacies proves that we may be certain of many things which are not necessarily true, and the widespread extent of such certainty is not of itself a logical proof— at least, not in the field of an exact science like mathematics or physics. Perhaps it is the subservience of logic to rhetoric (the art of disputation) that has caused us to look upon logical proof exclusively as a method of producing certainty or conviction. The essence of deduction or proof, however, is not the psychologic certainty which it may or may not produce, but the exhibition or demonstration of the logical structure of the system studied. The fact that a theorem about the sum of two sides of a triangle being greater than the third is derived from a Euclidean axiom does not add to its psychologic certainty; but it does reveal the structure of the Euclidean system in showing that in so far as that theorem is concerned no additional axiom is necessary.

Certainty is a primal need of the intellectual life. We all need some ground from which to start and on which to light after our short swallow flights of doubt and critical reflection. Some walk with firmer foot in answering the question: What facts exist? and some in answering the question: What claims are valid? Logically, however, existence and validity are strictly correlative. We must admit certain things to exist because their claims are valid, and claims are valid because things exist. The existence of the logical or relational structure of Euclidean geometry is as much a fact as the composition of albumen, the structure of rocks, or the constitution of the solar system, all of which depend on geometric relations. But if the distinction between logic and physics as indicated above is valid, it is well to distinguish between logical relations which are necessary, and factual relations which are contingent. This distinction may be made in two ways: First, particular sciences like physics may be said to start with material assumptions; i.e., assumptions true only of certain objects, namely, entities occupying time and space, while logic assumes only laws applicable to all possible objects. The second way of drawing the distinction is to say that while physics and other special sciences assume systems governed by laws the contraries of which are abstractly possible, logic deals with laws whose contraries are devoid of meaning or application to any possible determinate objects. The assumptions of even the most developed physical science, such as mechanics, can be shown to be sufficient, but cannot be proved necessary, since it is possible that some other hypothesis may explain the facts. But the assumption that the objects of physics and other sciences must conform to logic is necessary in the sense that without it no science at all can be constructed.

10. *The Logic of Non-existents*

Against the view that logic explores the realm of the possible and the necessary we have the extreme nominalism or empiricism of men like Hume, Mach, and Schiller, who deny the existence of objective necessary relations and reduce everything to a consideration of the actual existence of terms or impressions. This glorification of the category of existence and disparagement of the categories of possibility and necessity shows itself in its clearest form in Mach's contention that the world is given but once and that it is not valid to argue as to what would have happened if things were different. Mr. Schiller is a loyal disciple of Mr. Bradley in his distrust of abstractions. M. Brunschvicg, in a recent book, thinks it a triumphant argument against the new logical realism that it is as applicable to the world of Poe's imagination as to the real world of science.

The error underlying this view is as profound as it is widespread. The category of reality belongs not to science but to religion. It arises not as an aid to an intellectual analysis of our world, but as a means of escape or deliverance from the perplexities and confusions of deceitful appearances in a disorderly world. At any rate, it is rather easy to show that the prejudice in favor of reality (and the special form of it which glorifies the category of existence) is based on an inadequate analysis of the nature of science. Science would be impossible if we could not study the consequences of materially false hypotheses. In all sciences the consequences of rival hypotheses, such as those concerning the ether, must be deduced irrespective of their material truth, and indeed as a necessary condition before the material truth can be determined. Though two contradictory hypotheses cannot both be true in the material or existential sense, both must be assumed to have determinate consequences.

The realm of science cannot, therefore, be restricted to the realm of actual or historic existence. Indeed, determinate existence without any reference to possibility would be meaningless in mundane affairs. Science studies the character or determinate properties of things, whether actual or possible. In this respect science, like art and practical effort, liberates us from the prison-house of the actual and enables us to penetrate beyond to the region of the possible. What we call ideals or hypotheses are our guides in the labyrinth of possibility. The positivists who boast that they are concerned only with what is, like the hard-hearted statesmen or businessmen who say that they deal only with hard actualities, are deluding themselves with fantastical dogmas, hiding the crudity of their ideals with the pretense that they have none.

11. *Logic and Induction*

We have used the term *logic* or *formal logic* as identical with deduction. But as modern textbooks on logic devote more and more attention to what they call methodology and induction, a few remarks on these subjects are called for.

Though the term *method* is one of the most frequently used,

it is one of the least frequently defined terms in the whole reper-
tory of philosophy. It is, therefore, best to examine what is
actually treated under the head of methodology, and this I think
will always be found to fall under one of the following heads:

1. Elementary ideas or general principles, culled from the
various special sciences, and stated perhaps in a more abstract
and uniform language than in the books professing to deal with
these special sciences directly (e.g., Bain's *Logic*).

2. An account of the psychologic processes involved in scientific thought, i.e., in the process of learning or scientific demonstration (e.g., Sigwart and his followers).

3. Historical information as to the way certain great scientific
discoveries are supposed to have been made.

4. Directions as to how science is to be cultivated so as to
lead to discovery of laws or causes.

Of these the first three may be auxiliary to pure logic but
certainly outside of its proper domain, while the fourth is entirely beyond its competence.

Though the idea of logic as an organon or aid in discovery
seems to be as ancient as the science of logic itself, it does not
seem to me that this claim can be seriously supported on behalf
of either the ancient Aristotelian or the modern Baconian logic.
In the main it is true enough that a knowledge of truths already
known is the principal condition for the discovery of new ones,
and the knowledge of any science may thus indirectly help in
the exploration of any other field; but the science which will
teach everyone to become a discoverer of new laws has not yet
been found, and the student of logic as such seems (if we judge
by past experience) to be the least likely to find it. The logician
cannot pretend to be able to act as intellectual physician or
trainer to the scientific specialist. He may at best, if he takes the
unusual trouble of familiarizing himself thoroughly with the
subject matter of the various sciences, act a part similar to that
of the analytic critic of literature—he may indicate significant
identities and differences in the various sciences and criticize
the adequacy of the evidence for certain general contentions.

Such a comparative logical study would, if developed, be of inestimable value, but it would belong to applied rather than pure logic.

On the subject of induction I can but repeat the statement made some years ago by Bertrand Russell, that all inference is deductive and that what passes as induction is either disguised deduction or more or less methodical guesswork.

This statement has shocked many logicians who do not like to admit that in science as in other fields of life guessing or anticipations can play a part. But it is to be noted that the fact that a proposition is arrived at by a process of guessing does not determine its truth or falsity nor the purely logical question of its relation to other propositions. It is therefore absurd to draw a sharp antithesis between induction as a method of discovery and deduction as a method of exposition. Deductive logic and pure mathematics generally deal with certain relations between propositions, and the knowledge of such relations is certainly one of the most potent instruments of scientific research.

A brief glance at some typical views of induction may perhaps make my meaning clearer.

The term *induction* has been used to denote among other things:

1. Reasoning from facts or particulars to laws or universals (Boethius and the scholastics).

2. Reasoning which is based on the principle of uniformity of nature, i.e., like effects must have like causes (Mill).

3. Disjunctive reasoning (Schuppe, Montague).[5]

1a. As to the first, we must start with the observation that science never draws any inference from any sense-data except when the latter are viewed as already embodying or illustrating certain universals. It would obviously be impossible to state what happened in a single laboratory experiment except in terms of abstract or universal properties, such as weight, velocity, change, etc. All generalization of this type omits some elements

[5] Schuppe, *Erkenntnistheorie*, p. 53 ff; Montague, "On the Nature of Induction," *Journal of Philosophy*, vol. 3, p. 281 ff.

of the specific in order to widen the range of application. This process is not as such logically determinate, since the part omitted or abstracted may vary. Consider, for instance, the case of a man falling out of a window to his death. The incident may be described in an indefinite number of ways: To the psychologist it may be a case of frustrated love leading to suicide; to the physiologist, the loss of life through a fracture of the skull; to the physicist, the crushing of a body by impact at high velocity with a harder body. Thus the passage from the concrete to the abstract may take varying forms among which logic does not arbitrate since all are legitimate in their place. There is, thus, in fact no rigorously determined passage from pure particulars to universals.

1*b*. If the sharp metaphysical separation between facts and laws is waived, and induction is defined as reasoning in which the end or conclusion is more general than the beginning or premises, this account of the matter is still untenable. In deductive geometry or algebra we can pass by strict deductive steps from the nature of triangles (e.g., in respect to area) to that of all polygons, or from the nature of integers to that of numbers generally (as in the binomial theorem).

2. Mill's account of induction makes it synonymous with reasoning by analogy. "This medicine cured my little girl, therefore it will cure yours." Now there can be no doubt that this is the way most people actually reason, in the sense that this is what they are conscious of as what goes on in their minds. But in truth the consequence follows from the premise only when your little girl is like mine in all respects in which the given medicine is applicable. Hence, as scientific medicine develops, the question whether their cases are alike comes to the foreground and the argument changes from a blind empiricism to an argument which tends to assume the explicitly deductive form.

3. The account of induction which makes it synonymous with disjunctive reasoning seems to me thoroughly sound and illuminating. In actual scientific inquiry we start with a number of merely or barely possible explanations. The cause of A may be

C, D, or E, or any other number of circumstances. If one of these hypotheses be true certain consequences should follow, and any failure of one of these consequences rules out the hypothesis and thus diminishes the number of alternatives. This explains how it may happen that a single experiment may lead to the elimination of all but one possibility and therefore the definitive establishment of a law.[6] From this point of view Mill's method of agreement and difference [7] has a limited usefulness as a method of eliminating the circumstances which are not causal, and thereby helping somewhat in finding the true cause. But it is to be observed that the efficiency of this method depends on our fundamental assumption as to what circumstances are relevant or possibly related causally to the given effect. If the true cause is not included in our major premise the "canons of induction" will not enable us to discover it. If anyone thinks that I have understated the case for these canons of induction as methods of discovery, let him discover by their means the cause of cancer or of disorders in internal secretions.

12. *Conclusion*

To sum up the position of this chapter: The field of every science consists of the relations of certain constants and variables. The constants need not be enduring substances but may be the invariant laws according to which the changes take place. If the actually formulated laws of our physics can be shown to undergo change themselves, it can only be in reference to something else which is constant in relation to them. This justifies the Kantian contention for *a priori* elements in experience, in the sense that every science must assume some invariant connections or categories. The Kantians, however, are wrong in claiming absolute

[6] This is the *schema* of a crucial experiment. In the actual history of science things are more complicated, and none of the historical instances of crucial experiments given in the logic books were in fact as decisive as the books pretend.

[7] The method of residues is simply the disjunctive syllogism over again.

logical necessity for material principles such as those of Euclid's geometry, Newton's mechanics or Christian ethics. These principles are assumptions which may be necessary for some of the consequences drawn from them, but they are not absolutely necessary, since it is possible to reject these consequences. This view agrees with the experimental theory of knowledge and morals, except so far as the latter seems to repeat Hume's denial of objectively necessary relations or rules. Without the latter there can be no rational experiment or significant doubt.

II

Propositions and Uncompleted Symbols

Propositions have been treated linguistically as declarative sentences, psychologically as judgments, and logically as that which is true or false. The division of intellectual workers into grammarians, psychologists and logicians has tended to make us treat these supplementary modes of approach as if they were mutually exclusive. And this tendency to emphasize one element to the exclusion of others shows itself in the strife between nominalists, conceptualists or mentalists, and logical realists.

1. *Propositions as Acts of Mind*

The prevailing view, up to recently, has regarded propositions as essentially judgments which are acts of individual minds. Though this, like its rival views, can be traced back to Aristotle, its chief modern impetus came from eighteenth century individualistic subjectivism (represented by Berkeley and Hume) and from the philosophy of Kant and his Romantic successors, in which the world was treated as a mental synthesis or construction. The latter point of view has naturally led to a form of coherence theory of truth in which the psychologic act of judgment is primary and the object judged has a derivative or secondary existence, if any. Exclusive attention to the act of judgment not only reduces the object to a minor or shadowy role, but fails to come to close grips with the nature or role of the linguistic expression.

It would be vain to deny the great contributions to logic from idealists such as Bradley. But many of these services have been independent of, and others have been despite, the attempted absorption of logic into psychology, empirical or transcendental. Thus Bradley's penetrating discrimination between premises and principles of inference was also made on realistic grounds by Peirce; and the former's fundamental distinction between the real and the ideal elements in judgment fits much better into a Platonic or logical realism such as is employed in the modern analysis of mathematical limits and of the ideal entities of physics, such as absolutely free or rigid bodies, frictionless motion, and the like. The truth is that while modern idealism has, since the days of Berkeley, been attacking materialism, it has, even in its absolutistic form, shared the nominalism of the latter in rejecting the reality of abstract universals.

In opposition to the materialistic view that the realm of meaning or significant reference must be restricted to the existence of natural bodies, two types of argument have been developed. The more ancient and genuinely idealistic one (which in a general way may be called Platonic) argues for the objective reality of universal ideas or ideals on the basis of the inadequacy of separate atomic bodies to form a truly existent and hence knowable world. The second one (represented in its most typical form by Berkeley) argues against the genuine existence of matter on the ground that the mind can have no universal ideas, and that matter is just such a universal idea. But if we are to deny the existence of matter because it is a universal, a similar argument applies against the existence of mind. But though this becomes clear in Hume, modern psychologism has insisted on restricting meaning to the purely mental realm. And when mind is thus identified with the conscious experience of individuals, logic becomes implicitly a description of how such individual minds work when they make judgments.

But what distinguishes true from false judgments? If the distinction depends, as we all do assume in our daily activities, on the nature of the things judged, then a logic that is concerned with the relation between propositions as regards their truth and falsity has to go beyond mere description of the way men actually do think. It has to take into account the objective order which renders false many of our actual judgments not in agreement with it.

The recognition of an objective order independent of our individual judgments and controlling their truth is not avoided by the doctrine of a transcendental self whose judgments do not merely recognize the true order of things, but create it. No more light is added to our knowledge as to how the world into which we are born was created, or as to the nature of its creator, by calling the latter our transcendental self or mind than by saying it is the act of Jehovah or Allah. Few, if any of us, would venture to say: I am the author of the heaven and earth and the fullness thereof. Is there any more justification for any of us to say: My mind has created the earth and the starry universe and all that has happened throughout time and space?

The basic fallacy of transcendentalism, for which the seed is to be found in Kant's deduction of the categories, is the confusion between the logical requirement that anything I call an object should have a possible "I" (like my own) that can think it, and the ontologic assertion that there exists an everlasting ego or self which is conscious of all that has existed and will exist because it creates everything. The latter proposition may possibly be true, but it does not follow from purely logical requirements. Nor can more be said for the argument that reifies the subject of all possible science into a ghostly "mind of humanity." Actual knowledge is something attained by particular human beings, in time and space, and possible knowledge is simply the bare possibility of this happening. It is vain to attempt by purely logical analysis of such possibility to prove the existence of anything over and above the natural world spread in time and space. But we need not for our present purposes examine the theologic or metaphysical sins of pantheism. If with an extreme idealist such as Schelling we explicitly admit that there is a difference between the transcendental and the empirical self, the judgments of the latter must, if they are true, conform to an order of things independent of them. Calling the latter, as well as the former, mental will not abolish their difference or change their relation.

There is not within the psychologic view of logic sufficient basis for rejecting the position of humanistic pragmatism, which in the interest of our volitions, faith or moral values, disparages all abstractions or invariant relations of nature that are norms or controls which we must follow if we wish to avoid error. In disregarding the invariant relations of the objective world which logic explores, F. C. S. Schiller follows Bradley's view of science as fictional and merely practical. But neither human will nor judgment creates the physical or biologic world, or even (by itself) the cultural institutions which mold us. We are effective only to the extent that we wisely recognize an order of existence independent of our likes or dislikes.

Psychologism may and often does take a dualistic rather than a monistic form. It assumes a world of nature in which there are individual things and a world of mind in which are located all abstractions and relations between things. To this view there are two objections, of which we may take brief note.

1. If relations can rightly be rejected from the objective world because they are abstractions, then particular objects or individuals apart from their relations are equally unreal because they are equally abstract. The world that we must assume in all intelligible discussion is a world of terms related in certain ways because of the nature of the objects studied or considered; and the progress of knowledge is a progress in the discovery of such relations. This is incompatible with the view that things exist in one world, that of nature, and relations in quite another, that of mind. And if we say all objects and their relations exist alike in the mind, the word *mind* ceases to have its original distinctive meaning, since it then covers everything and nothing distinctive.

2. If there is any difficulty about admitting the existence of relations in nature, that difficulty can in no way be cured by placing them in the mind. For Berkeley's argument against the

existence of universals and abstract "ideas" as definite images in the mind is unanswerable on a nominalistic or psychologic basis.

What may seem a metaphysically more neutral form of the coherence theory, regards any judgment as true if it coheres or agrees with all other judgments so as to form an all-comprehensive system, and false if it fails to do so. But while consistency is undoubtedly necessary it is not (by itself) sufficient to establish the categoric truth of any proposition, since all sorts of systems can be and have been built up on false premises. Granted that contradictory accounts of the same object or universal cannot both be true, it does not follow that the falsity of either account will show itself in the presence of contradictory judgments within it. We may have to resort to immediate experience which is not in itself a judgment, though it may give rise to one. In any case, since the meaning of a judgment is its reference to some state of affairs, that which determines consistency cannot be independent of the objects judged, and the latter need not be restricted to other judgments.

If we look at the matter somewhat more empirically, we are tempted to ask, "Does the act of judgment in fact always precede or accompany the statement of what we call a proposition?" It would be absurd to deny that people sometimes really think and judge before they speak or write; and it may be highly desirable that this should be more often the case, even though it would lead to a most painful reduction of pleasant learned and unlearned discourse. But to assert the dogma that every statement of a proposition is actually in fact nothing but the expression of an act of judgment on the part of the speaker or writer is surely to fly in the face of common experience. For not only are thoughtless assertions frequent, but few of us ever perceive the full meaning of the general propositions which we habitually assert.

Let us take an ordinary example. A friend says, "All men now violate the law." I ask him, "What! Do you mean that I am guilty of some crime?" And he replies with some embarrassment, "I do not mean you in particular." Shall I conclude that he wishes to insult me by denying my manhood? Would it not be more sensible, as well as more courteous, to assume that he did not realize the full meaning of what he said? If this example seems undignified, consider the case of a faculty or legislative committee that deliberates and drafts a rule. Who fully understands its meaning when it is enacted as a law? Experience amply shows that the authors are sometimes puzzled when some actual case comes up and they are asked to interpret the meaning of the rule which has resulted from their deliberations.

The truth is that the meaning of assertions is more than a matter of mere individual intention. In the history of every individual speech is prior to thought. The child learns to utter words before he learns to judge and discriminate their meanings. And in adult life if we do not know the meaning of a word we inquire or investigate, as we do in regard to any other fact. Moreover, in the history of the human race, organic response is prior to judgment in the development of speech. Our consciousness of meaning is, for the most part, a development of the consciousness of our organic attitudes or "sets" toward other objects. Much can be said for the view that an act of judgment is necessarily involved in apprehending the meaning of any proposition. But we must not confuse the meaning of a proposition with our conscious apprehension of that meaning. The meaning of a passage in Homer or in the Magna Carta no more depends upon my judgment than my own actual existence in the past is created by my present judgment.

Meaning in general is thus a relation between a thing and something else to which it points or refers. In this general sense a cloudy sky means the likelihood of rain and a given bone may mean the former existence of a carnivorous animal. One may well contend that a bone is a bone and does not mean anything except to a mind that has certain information and judges accordingly. But such information is about the real connection between things. The important point is that *what* anything means is in no wise created by our apprehension, but is presupposed by the latter.

Against this view it has been urged that since the same object might mean different things to different observers, meaning cannot be a trait of the object itself. But a more adequate view of meaning regards it as a triadic relation between (1) an object; (2) that to which it points; and (3) a conscious observer. Thus, a field of goldenrod may mean to some the beginning of our beautiful American autumn, while to others it may mean the coming of hay-fever. While this is true, we must not confuse relativity with subjectivity. If we distinguish between the organic human being and the mind as the subject of knowledge, we can see that the latter as percipient is not a term in the perceived relation even when the same object has different effects on different organisms. In general any object has meaning if it serves as a sign of, or refers to, something more than itself. The object need not be an existing one. It may be purely imaginary if it suggests something else, e.g., Venus or Aphrodite. Even an impossible object may have meaning if it serves to call to mind other things than itself, e.g., a griffin or perpetual motion. The latter term has meaning because it calls to mind something definite, although impossible.

This will enable us to deal also with the argument that the meaning of a proposition is purely subjective because there is always a certain conventional element in language. We can, to a very limited extent, like Humpty-Dumpty, make words mean what we please. But all convention presupposes communication in a form which is ultimately not conventional but grows out of the fact that the communicants live in a common world and respond in similar ways to similar symbols. If Columbus makes himself intelligible to the West Indians, it is because the signs or gestures which he makes bring the results he expects, and his response to similar utterances on the part of the Indians brings them similar satisfaction which they manifest to him. It is impossible even to discover our misunderstandings except on the basis of a common world which makes possible better mutual understanding.

Even more obvious should all this be in the case of communi

cation through an established language, such as English, which
has not been created by any individual or group of individuals
living at any one time but has grown in the experience of count-
less generations. No one individual can by his volition change
its rules of syntax, though some grammarians, especially those
ignorant of the history of the English language, have caused certain idiomatic phrases to disappear (e.g., the old English expression, "up and at 'em," or the phrase, "except he"). Though language is a human fact, it is as objective as the air and the buildings that surround us in our cities. Linguistic forms may change
but they are relatively among the most constant of social facts.

Propositions then are not mere psychologic acts of judgment
independent of their linguistic expression or of a world beyond
them. It is extremely doubtful whether any of us do really ever
make judgments without the use of some linguistic medium. And
it would be absurd to base exact logic, as the most rigid weighing of evidence, upon insecure introspective evidence. We conclude, then, that propositions are linguistic forms with meanings
that are objective relations between such forms and certain states
of fact. Acts of judgment, however, are involved in the apprehension of those relations that are called meanings.

2. *Propositions as Meaningful Symbols*

The movement of logical realism which has come from the
study of mathematics and exact science has rightly emphasized
the objective state of affairs asserted in every proposition. This
has restored a precision and clarity to the field of logic which
we may without disparagement call "scholastic." But in its reaction against the absolutism of ineffable monism, it has fallen into
pluralistic absolutism or atomism which does little justice to the
relativity of meaning. It is well to speak of *gold is yellow* or
Jones gave a book to his mother as propositions of a definite
sort. But neither of these can be regarded as having a complete
meaning except in reference to the context or universe in which
they occur. Their truth or falsity holds only when their meaning

is thus completed. *Gold is yellow* sounds simple enough but what it means is an integrated part of, and depends upon, a very complex world. We cannot, therefore, tell whether it is true unless we have an adequate account of what gold is, what is yellow, and under what conditions it is that the latter holds true of the former. Thus, gold is not yellow except when it is in a certain light. That qualification is necessary to make our expression true and without it we have an incomplete symbol which is sometimes true and sometimes false according to the way we complete it. When not thus completed it is neither true nor false and therefore not a proposition at all.

Moreover, there are expressions like those about the King of France, generally regarded as false propositions, for which there is no sufficient reason to suppose that the nature of things will ultimately either show them to be true or show them to be false. A great many people are thoroughly and profoundly convinced that there is a present King of France, such as the Duke de Guise. Are the facts in the case such as to determine that this judgment is false? It is conceivable that the two parties on this issue might ultimately agree on all the purely existential facts in the case and still differ as to whether it is true or false that the Duke de Guise is the King of France, for one party may be resolved to adhere to the principle of legitimacy and the other party equally determined to accept the Republican decrees of expulsion as decisive. Both parties might then be perfectly well informed, perfectly consistent and yet continue to differ. Is it then a proposition to assert that there is not a present King of France? Obviously, there are many other expressions of the same propositional form which may turn out to be resolutions which the logicians generally do not regard as either always true or always false. We seem therefore to be left in the unsatisfactory state of talking about propositions and yet never being able to identify one with certainty. If so, how can we assert that there *are* propositions? Yet the whole procedure of Russell's *Principles of Mathematics* and of the *Principia Mathematica* clearly presupposes the existence of propositions of which examples are given. Can we avoid this difficulty by resorting to the device of interpreting all such expressions as formal: if p is a proposition then p implies, etc.? We cannot. For the latter assertion itself claims to be a proposition. Indeed, Mr. Russell himself, following Lewis Carroll, has clearly indicated the limitation of the principle of formalism [1] and has used the paradox of Lewis Carroll to prove the impossibility of dispensing with all categoric assertions.

The difficulty, however, is one which follows only for those who, like Lotze and the neo-Hegelians, ignore the distinction between formal and material knowledge (because of their acceptance of the nominalistic dogma that abstractions are unreal). On the principle of polarity there is no difficulty in admitting that certain verbal forms express or symbolize meanings that are never materially completed and yet have their conditions indicated, just as are the conditions of an infinite series of which we can tell definitely whether any proposed term does or does not belong to it, though we cannot have all the terms before us.

Granting that all propositions are true or false only in their ultimate ideal completion, we may look at their actual appearance and function which can be symbolized. We need not be frightened by the disparaging connotation of "merely verbal" or "merely linguistic." Nothing is a symbol, such as is a word, or a proposition, unless it is taken, not as an entity in itself, but as meaning, signifying, or pointing to something more than itself. Such meaning may be a matter of endless study and in that sense exists only formally or virtually in the eternal present, to be seen only by the mind's eye that is properly trained. But a logical realism can well be applied to, or be united with, such studies in the historical, social, and psychologic nature of language as have come in recent years from Wundt, Jesperson, and Sapir. The work of Charles Peirce shows some of the possibilities of philosophic grammar and should serve to revive interest in it.

What, now, distinguishes a proposition from other significant

[1] Russell, *Principles of Mathematics*, pp. 34-36.

objects or symbols? It is usual to regard a proposition as an ordered group of words, the order being expressed by inflection or
sequence. But a single word *cogito* or *ambulo* is clearly sufficient.
The analysis of propositions into *S is P* or *aRb* is often illuminating, but not always fitting. Sometimes it is forced. Mr. Russell makes the distinction between a proposition such as *John
walks* and the term *John walking* to consist in that the former
asserts something. What is the nature of logical as distinguished
from psychological assertion? For the sake of brevity let me say
dogmatically that it is *location—John's walking* is an unlocated
complex. When it is put into a time series it becomes *John
walked* or *John is walking.* Some languages like the Chinese
often dispense with verbs, but the location is then indicated
either by the order of the words or by intonation. When a child
says *Moon,* the mother may understand the child from its tone
or from its pointing as expressing the proposition, *this is the
moon.* The demonstrative is supplied by gesture.

If such location of an object in some universe is what we mean
by existence in general, then propositions assert existence while
concepts or terms merely denote or name essences.

The objective theory of the meaning of propositions has been
generally rejected on the ground that it does not fit the nature,
(1) of negative judgments, (2) of true assertions about non-exist-
ing or logically impossible entities, and (3) of false propositions.

The assumption that a negative proposition cannot refer directly to the objective world but involves the rejection of a suggested idea in our mind, is based on a confusion. There is no
valid reason for the denial that negative and positive judgments
are correlative. The judgment that certain lines are parallel is
ordinarily regarded as positive. But if we substitute *do not inter-
sect* for the term *parallel,* we have a negative judgment. Clearly,
there is no difference in objectivity between saying *Only the
brave deserve the fair,* or *All who deserve the fair are brave,* and
saying *Those who are not brave are undeserving of the fair. Undeserving* and *unworthy* may be viewed as very positive facts,

sometimes very poignantly so. The source of error in Bradley [2] and Bosanquet [3] on this point is that they select their negative judgments from a special type, namely, those that have for their immediate object not a state of fact but a personal judgment. Similarly erroneous is the notion that all negative judgments are essentially indefinite. The error here arises from the fact that when we affirm a complex proposition we affirm every part of it, while to deny such a proposition is to assert a number of alternatives, which seems less definite. But there is nothing inherently indefinite or indeterminate about the assertions of alternatives, and no less about positive than about negative ones. In a limited universe of discourse, such as the months of the year, an assertion about those that do not have thirty-one days is as definite as one about those that have thirty days or one or two less. Negative judgments are indefinite only when our universe of discourse is unlimited. A false proposition must have meaning in order to be false. This means, according to our analysis, that it asserts a possible universe, but is false because it is not compossible or compatible with the universe of actual existence, and that the former cannot be located within the latter. Thus, propositions which are true within a specified universe, for example, in the Homeric Pantheon, may not be true when taken in the universe which we call the real or physical one. The relativity here, let us note, is not subjective.

3. Interpretation

The point of view indicated in this essay suggests an important but neglected set of real problems, namely, those of hermeneutics. A study of the rules for determining what a given statement means is of importance not only to the philologist, including the historian, who must interpret documents, but also to the theologian and the lawyer, as well as the ordinary man or woman in the business of living—to all, that is, who are con-

[2] Bradley, *Principles of Logic,* vol. 1, bk. 1, chap. 3.
[3] Bosanquet, *Logic,* vol. 1, bk. 1, chap. 7.

cerned with the vital question of what some utterance means. Even theologians have tried to develop methodic rules in order to eliminate strained and arbitrary heretical interpretations; and Roman as well as Hebrew and English lawyers have worked at rules for determining the meaning of legal propositions. It is a provoking question as to how far, if at all, these rules enable us to get at the actual intentions behind the theologic or the legal text. But logic alone will not solve material problems. It is sufficient if it calls attention to their nature and indicates the kind of evidence necessary or sufficient for such solution.

III

Meaning and Implication

Though the rules which distinguish valid from invalid inference, the core of the traditional logic, can be formulated with mathematical rigor and precision, the precise scope of logic as a whole has not been very clear. Considering the vast amount of writing on logic, there has been a marked neglect to deal explicitly and adequately with the basic question as to whether it is about being, thought, or language.

There can be no doubt that as a technique modern symbolic logic has in recent times made fruitful advances beyond the power of the old rules of the syllogism. The history of science, however, shows that periods of great expansion and technical improvement, such, for instance, as prevailed in eighteenth-century mathematics or nineteenth-century biology, may be associated with loose or vague ideas as to philosophic fundamentals. The founder of logic as a special study treated it not only as an organon, or, as we should say, a calculus, but also as a part of metaphysics or ontology.[1] Its fundamental laws, those of identity, contradiction and excluded middle, he formulated as laws of being: Whatever is, is; nothing can both be and not be, etc. But as a result of the modern tendency to ignore ontologic issues in favor of psychologic ones, the view has prevailed since the beginning of the nineteenth century that logic was a branch of mental science, a study of how the mind works in the processes of conception, judgment and inference. Lipps summed up the

[1] See Aristotle, *Metaphysics*, Book Gamma.

modern tradition of Mill, Lotze, Sigwart, Bradley, Wundt, and
Creighton, in the statement that "Logic is a psychological discipline, as certainly as knowledge occurs only in the Psyche, and
thought, which is developed in knowledge, is a psychical event." [2]
Assuming this, critics such as F. C. S. Schiller, complained that
it was not sufficiently psychologic, that it did not describe how
men actually do think. The revelation of the close kinship between logic and mathematics, and the shifting of emphasis to
objective categories such as classes, order, series, and material
implication, at first strengthened or revivified the old Platonic
view of the reality of universals, and weakened the subjective
nominalism common both to the followers of Hume and to the
neo-Hegelians who had harped on the unreality of abstractions.
This realistic note may be seen not only in G. E. Moore's *Principia Ethica* and in Russell's *Principles of Mathematics* and
other of his earlier writings, but even more significantly in the
later works of Josiah Royce. In Europe, Meinong's *Gegenstands-
theorie* was developed by way of reaction to Hume's nominalistic treatment of relations; and Husserl's phenomenology with
its insistence that character or essence is not to be regarded as
merely subjective, grew out of his early preoccupation with the
logic of arithmetic and his criticism of Frege. Here in America
not only did our neo-realists participate in this revived recognition of the reality of universals, but even as anti-Germanic a
critical realist as Santayana, recognized his kinship with Husserl
in regard to the objectivity of essences.

Today, however, we see everywhere signs of an emphatic return to an extreme nominalism, which reduces logic and pure
mathematics to mere linguistic devices, and claims to have demonstrated thereby the essential meaninglessness of ethical and
metaphysical questions.

To those acquainted with the nominalist tradition from Sex-
tus Empiricus and Hume to Mach and Fritz Mauthner, there is,
to be sure, little novelty in the substance of this contention. It

[2] Lipps, *Grundzüge der Logik*, pp. 1-2.

has, however, found some new support in the symbolic view of mathematics elaborated by the school of Hilbert and in the work of the Polish logicians on semantics and on the theory of language. Its hold on many of our younger philosophers is shown by the extent to which the grammatical term *sentence* is replacing the logical term *proposition*.

Without attempting any systematic treatment of the problems involved, I wish to advance some considerations as to why formal or mathematical logic cannot entirely dispense with the categories of meaning and implication and to urge that it thus cannot be reduced to psychology or to linguistics, but must have general ontologic reference.

1. *Meaning and Formal Logic*

Judged by its crucial importance for the solution of all sorts of theoretic and practical issues, the precise nature of meaning has received relatively scant attention. It is not surprising to find such neglect on the part of professional linguists, that is, men whose primary interest lies in amassing detailed knowledge of many languages. Their business in amassing the requisite amount of detailed information naturally leaves them little energy for theoretic reflection. Besides, it has been observed that few professional linguists are found among philosophers. It seems, as some contend, that preoccupation with sounds and words dulls the edge of speculation.

More surprising is the fact that grammarians as a rule have failed to give the question of meaning adequate and explicit attention. But grammarians have been proverbially pedagogues, and, as a professional class, not distinguished by keen intellectual virility. The business of training young people makes them naturally respecters of authority and convention. This shows itself in their studious aversion to considering the language spoken by the great majority of their fellow men. English grammars refuse to consider English as spoken by Cockneys or other members of the so-called vulgar multitude. Good or grammatical English usage is set by a minority who are in a position of authority because of the possession of wealth, high office, or other distinction. In recent times a few bold spirits have ventured to assert the obvious truth that the main purpose of language is to make oneself understood and that the success in effecting such understanding is the main test of the goodness of any language. This view, however, meets an insuperable obstacle in the pervasive and deep-rooted snobbishness of mankind.

Language, after all, is a form of conduct. All people try to imitate their "betters." And as education is, in the main, the privilege of the wealthier classes who can afford to send their children to school for the relatively long period demanded by grammarians, good speech thus becomes the mark of the wealthier classes or of those who are specially privileged through church connections or otherwise.

Quite recently there has been a growing interest in grammar as a purely scientific study. But what such scientific students think of the conventional grammar taught in our schools is indicated by Professor Brunot, who writes as follows:

> Incomprehensible abstractions, pretentious yet for the most part empty definitions, false rules, indigestible lists of forms—one has only to turn over a few pages of any text book to find variegated specimens of sins against reason, truth and education.[3]

More surprising still is the fact that a thorough study of the problem of meaning has not come from logicians. This is probably to be explained by the fact that the traditional logic has

[3] From *L'Enseignement de la Langue Française*, p. 3, quoted in Ogden and Richards, *The Meaning of Meaning* (1923), p. 392.

The French are notorious in taking pride in cultivating their language, so that the situation is much worse as regards English grammar, which has been treated as a step-child among the grammarians themselves, who have been trained to regard Latin as the only grammar and therefore have neglected almost entirely a study of English up to very recently. See Lists of Sins in English Grammar in chapter 5 of G. Willis' *The Philosophy of Speech* (1919).

not kept close touch with the facts of language, and logicians have unguardedly fallen under the influence of the traditional school grammars. This is illustrated by the uncritical use of the conventional categories such as noun, article, and the like, employed by Carnap in his *Logical Syntax*. In Russell's *Principles of Mathematics* there is, to be sure, an application of purely logical considerations to the traditional grammatical categories. But that phase of Russell's work has had relatively little influence.

A realization that logic is a part of science and not the whole of it, that it cannot pretend to settle questions of truth and falsity in all realms, has led to the view that it deals only with the forms of thought. Are we, however, offered a clear idea as to how the forms of thought differ from its content, or what indeed the former are apart from the latter? The whole distinction between form and content when applied to a mental operation turns out to be a rather obscure metaphor. Nor does the modern concept of method by itself clarify the issue if we realize how inept and futile logicians are in dealing with the methods of any science when they are not fully informed as to its subject matter. Logic is thus faced with a dilemma. Either its subject matter is all truth and it is thus indistinguishable from the body of all the sciences and true knowledge, or else it is formal in the sense of being entirely empty. And how can that which is empty of all content have any meaning?

At this point those who call themselves logical positivists boldly take the truly nihilistic position that formal logic deals with linguistic expressions without any reference to sense or meaning.[4] In view of the great vogue which this school has attained, partly because of its obvious virtuosity in dealing with strictly technical issues and partly, I venture to add, because it is often easier to manipulate symbols than to consider carefully what it is that they symbolize—it has been remarked that the pencil on paper or chalk on the board is often more reliable than the man who

[4] Carnap, *Logical Syntax of Language*, pp. 1-8.

uses it, and that is why he resorts to it—it is important to guard against two errors in its position. These are: (1) that we can treat language or symbols apart from all meaning, and (2) that there is no difference between logical and merely linguistic considerations.

1. No one, I take it, wishes to deny that the intelligible communication of something or other is essential to language and that this excludes meaningless sounds or marks. Can we, therefore, speak of linguistic expressions where there is no sense or meaning? And can inferences be drawn from that which is quite meaningless? One is led to give an affirmative answer to both of these questions if one accepts the view that logic is concerned with linguistic expressions and is formal in the sense of being devoid of all reference to meaning. Professor Carnap defends the position that logical inference is independent of meaning by an example: From *Pirots karulize elatically* and *A is a Pirot,* we can infer that *A karulizes elatically,* without knowing the meaning of the three words or the sense of the three sentences. He admits however that these are sentences only because we assume that *Pirots* is a substantive, *karulize* is a verb (both of these terms are plural in the first sentence and singular in the others) and *elatically* is an adverb describing a way in which a process takes place. These expressions are therefore not entirely meaningless as would be undiluted gibberish. If instead of *Pirots* we put *"the members of any class of objects"* and instead of *karulize elatically* we put *are members of another class* we have as an inference that *a member of the first class is necessarily a member of the second class.* And this I submit is the actual meaning which Professor Carnap's example suggests to anyone to whom the inference seems a valid one. This statement applies to all possible objects irrespective of any of their specific or differential traits but assuredly is not therefore entirely meaningless.

While engaged in manipulating his symbols the mathematician or symbolic logician need not be concerned with any particular meaning or interpretation of his p's and q's, though he must be sure that in his manipulation he is not illogical but employs his rules of operation with logical consistency.[5] But there is an obvious distinction between the science of mathematics and the art of arranging pebbles according to certain rules or patterns or playing a childish game such as tick-tack-toe. For though science as a human activity may well be called an art, it is of its essence that its statements should be applicable to some realm of nature; and, to be so, the sounds or marks which it employs must have some objective reference. If, therefore, our p's and q's, horseshoes or other marks were nothing but objects like pebbles, or the crosses and circles of tick-tack-toe, it would be difficult to see how mathematics could be the primary science and such an indispensable instrument in the discovery of physical and other truths which are surely more than merely linguistic.

The operations of mathematics are in fact significant because they apply not only to the marks actually used but to all possible objects. Just as the particular diagrams in Euclid are not the true objects of the demonstration but only aids to our imagination to help us envisage the possible entities to which they can be applied, so do the various letters and other marks enter logic and mathematics, not in their status as specific physical objects, but rather as representatives of all possible entities. A mathematical statement has in this way reference beyond the immediate sounds or marks that enter it. It is, of course, essential for a logical or purely mathematical system that it be formal in the sense of being independent of any particular embodiment or interpretation, but that does not mean that it must be devoid of all reference to sense and truth. In the latter case it would be an empty, meaningless and frivolous enterprise. Truth or falsity, however, can be genuinely applied to inferences or mathematical

[5] For the laws of identity, contradiction and excluded middle are assumed or involved in any game or operational calculus. Any attempt to prove or derive them from other propositions must involve the assumption that our p's and q's remain the same throughout our calculation and that in any given context one or other of these given symbols does or does not properly belong.

operations, according as the latter involve statements as to what does or does not follow or what is or is not possible within any system of transformations.

2. The now popular view that logic and pure mathematics are merely linguistic, i.e., deal only with words and their arrangements in sentences, rests on a confusion between a truism and a falsehood. It is a truism that logic determines what combinations of words are meaningless because devoid of logical consequences. It is false that logic and mathematics are about words only, in the sense that they are in no way concerned with the world which words denote or to which they point or refer. Apart from such possible denotation we do not have any words or sentences at all but only physical objects; and the manipulation of the latter would be an exercise in acoustics or optics, and in no way linguistic. Those who insist on the linguistic nature of mathematics seem not only to be misled by this ambiguous character of verbal symbols, but to have fallen into the common fallacy of false alternatives. Language and the objects which language indicate are properly distinguishable, but it does not follow that their relation is one of mutual exclusion. Language itself involves physical, physiologic, psychologic and social-historic factors as well as purely logical considerations, and no absolute division between sentences about objects and sentences about words can be maintained, since words are also objects and meaningless sounds or marks do not properly constitute sentences. Moreover logic and mathematics cannot be reduced to merely linguistic considerations. Lexicography or semantics as a branch of linguistic science is a description or account of what given physical sounds or visible marks have generally denoted under certain historical conditions among Germans, Romans, Turks, Bushmen or others. But we do not expect to solve all the problems of mathematics or logic, any more than the problems of physics, by merely consulting a dictionary, valuable or even indispensable as the information in the latter may be. Logic and mathematics are concerned not with the specific or physical ele-

ments or their historical relation to the things they denote but with the most generally or abstractly possible relations between all objects of denotation. When we deduce the consequences of certain premises in geometry or rational mechanics, we are not primarily concerned with the dictionary meaning of words, though that may be a condition of speech. We are dealing with certain consequences of that to which words point.

It is well known that languages have phonetically lazy or inactive letters, such as *ugh* in English in the word "thorough," or *ent* in French, and similar forms. In the same way languages have linguistically silent words, such as the word *now* in the sentence, "Now at that time there was a certain man," or the Greek *men* and *de,* sometimes called "enclitic." These words fulfill the function of filling out the sound or volume of speech, for speech has its own volume apart from the meaning. These and other reasons indicate why the syntax of words cannot correspond fully to the meaning. There is no one-to-one correspondence between words and the things which words denote, and much less is that the case between words and ideas or thoughts. Syntax is indeed the most idiomatic aspect of language. Every language has a peculiar syntax as shown by the difficulty of learning to speak or write another language without falling into ridiculous errors. This is forcibly illustrated by Mark Twain in his literal translation of the French version of the story of the "Jumping Frog." Indeed people generally have more difficulty acquiring the syntax than acquiring the vocabulary. The question whether a given proposition proves another is surely not a purely linguistic one; it is not settled entirely by a knowledge of the grammar or syntax of any given language, but depends upon what is asserted, so that we can correctly translate from one language to another without affecting the validity or cogency of any proof.

If scientific proof in mathematics, physics or any other science depended on the syntax of any language such as German, Arabic, or Turkish, then there could be no universal science, but only German, Arabic, or Turkish sciences or logics.

2. *The Nature of Meaning*

To see more clearly the relation between linguistics, physics and logic we must distinguish three kinds of meaning: (1) verbal meaning as the denotation of words,[6] (2) material meaning, or the nature of things which we wish to understand, as when we ask for the meaning of the present rise or fall of prices, and (3) purely logical implication, which enables us to pass from premises to conclusions irrespective of whether the former are in fact true or false.

Nominalism may be identified with the assumption that verbal meaning is primary, and the other forms are metaphoric or derivative. This seems to me untenable on linguistic as well as on logical grounds.

Let us note at the outset that words are not primary or essential to language, if by the latter we mean significant communication, i.e., expressions which are understood by the speaker or writer in the same way as by the hearer or reader. We can communicate without words by gesture and in other ways such as by drawing pictures. The gesture is not only the primitive form of language but is still a necessary part of it, as can be seen in watching people talk. Indeed, how else can the meaning of words be ultimately indicated except by some arrangement which will enable us to associate the words with the thing or operation pointed to or indicated? Public orators are not the only ones who would be seriously handicapped if they were not able to move their arms or their facial muscles. Many things which otherwise cannot be adequately expressed can be more fully indicated by appropriate gesture or tone of voice. Indeed, words become definite only by being used in sentences, or when associated with an object through organic communication such as demonstrative gesture, pantomime, or variations of tone and stress. The adult life of scholars or bookish people is so much engaged in

[6] I use the word "denotation" in the broad sense to include what Mill calls "connotation."

written language and in putting words together, that it fosters
the illusion that words are the basic or primary elements of language. A little reflection on the way a child learns to communicate its wishes or desires, or the way the incomparable Charlie
Chaplin communicates many things which amuse us, indeed the
way in which even brute animals generally communicate their
desires, shows clearly that verbal meaning is derivative and presupposes some recognition of a common world.

Unless two individuals recognize the same objects, they cannot
have common symbols. When we translate from German into
English or from sign language into speech, what is the test of
the equivalence of the expressions, if it is not that they denote
or point to the same object? The perception of the material
meaning or nature of the object symbolized is therefore essential
to the recognition of verbal equivalence. Thus, children begin
by using the same word regularly for many different things; and
it is only through the fact that they fail to communicate their
wants or to attain their objectives that the meaning of words gets
more defined.

That complete definiteness of denotation is seldom attained
for any word by itself is obvious on an examination of any
scholarly dictionary which enumerates its different meanings.
But dictionaries gather only the main types of meaning. The
subtler shades which the same word can have in different contexts evade attempts at exhaustive description or enumeration.
It may not be true, as was alleged by Spencer, that the members
of certain tribes cannot understand each other in the dark; but
it is certainly true that without the proper intonation, you cannot communicate in Chinese. Even in English the meaning of
such a sentence as, *If he slay me, yet will I trust him,* is completely altered by a rising inflection, as in the sentence, *Oh, yes.*
Syntax, while not irrelevant to meaning, may thus be a poor
guide to it. That it is the context of the objective situation that
gives definite meaning to our words, is seen in the fact that we
often can tell in reading a passage what word has been left out.
The more we are familiar with the subject matter, the easier it is

to interpret the meaning or text; and if we are unfamiliar with a subject matter, e.g., Roman law, we may fail to understand a sentence even though the meaning of every word is defined in our dictionary. In general, knowledge of the meaning of all the words in a sentence may be inadequate to give the meaning of the sentence. This can readily be seen in translating from one language to another. Now if we fix our attention on the actual process by which words acquire meaning, or, more generally, on the way objects become signs or symbols, we find that such objects are originally parts of larger situations or complexes, and their meaning is their pointing to or representing something beyond themselves. Thus, the sound *moon* acquires its meaning in a situation in which it is accompanied by the gesture of pointing to the earth's illumined satellite. So the sound *more* gets to be significant if it is accompanied by an increase of food or some other desired addition. And from the point of view of this analysis, any physiological symptom or physical sign has meaning. Thus rapid breathing means a weakening of the heart which will show itself in the pulse; and similarly a heavy cloud or a certain state of the barometer means rain.

In actual common discourse we do often use the term *meaning* as synonymous with the *nature of things;* as when we speak of the meaning of economic crises, or anything else which we wish to understand. Thus, Ogden and Richards might properly have called their book *The Nature of Meaning* instead of *The Meaning of Meaning.* Many, to be sure, find it difficult to agree that a heavy cloud can literally mean rain. They regard such an expression as metaphorical. But every metaphor is an implicit analogy, and any two things can be analogous only if they have some common element, relation or pattern. May we not then say that anything acquires meaning if it is connected with, or indicates, or refers to, something beyond itself, so that its full nature points to and is revealed in that connection? Preoccupation with introspective psychologic considerations leads us so to emphasize intuition as to consider it the essential element of all meaning. But such a view is not necessary.

3. Words and Sentences

The last point brings us to the consideration of the relation between words and sentences.

Professor Carnap *seems* to reduce logic, mathematics and metaphysics to syntactical sentences, which he contrasts sharply with sentences about objects. I do not pretend to understand him, for I cannot see how logical and mathematical statements, if they are characterized as devoid of sense or meaning, can also be true or false. Nor do I understand what difference, if any, he draws between logical and linguistic syntax. But to any suggestion that words denoting objects are primary and that the meaning of sentences results from the synthesis of the meaning of words, we must reply that this is an illusion, that in fact words are more or less arbitrary fragments into which purely conventional usage breaks up phrases or clauses. Commonly recognized sentences like "Come," or "Go," the Latin "Veni," or "Cogito," or the Greek "Γράφω," or our interrogative "Well?" do not seem to result from any synthesis of different words. But it is not necessary to settle this point or the interminable controversies among philologists as to what precisely is a word and what is a sentence. It is sufficient for logical purposes to note that any analysis of what is commonly called a sentence into words fails to exhaust its meaning and is not a very reliable guide to it. It is the fallacy of reduction to suppose that a phrase or sentence is equivalent to the words that compose it.

Doubtless, uninflected languages like English are great aids in the analysis of objective meaning. But it is well to insist that not only is the primary force in the development of language practical or organic rather than noetic or analytic of ideas, but that purely phonetic considerations, arbitrary symbols, customs and their habitual analogies enter into the verbal sentence structure of all languages. For this reason, the syntactical rules of any human language can never be purely logical. Grammatically, *good, potential, former, existing,* are all adjectives when applied to the noun *king,* but in meaning they move on quite different levels. Is the notion of the future more complex than the notion of the past simply because we can express past action by one word (I) *saw,* whereas the future requires at least two, (I) *will see,* and sometimes more, as (I) *am going to see?* Doubtless "I have a pain" or "I am in pain" is more analytical than the more primitive "Ouch," but it would be misleading if we took the *in* of "I am in pain" or the *have* in the expression "I have a pain," as essential parts of the meaning which we wish to convey. We say, "I have money in my pocket," "I have to go home," and the French say, "I have wrong." Can we say that the "have" in these cases is of any aid in the analysis of the real meaning of our sentence? That is the error of those who identify words with the elements of meaning.

Words form a discreet linear series, but what any assemblage of them denotes may be continuous, and often is so. Any syntax must arrange words in order of "nextness," but things or states of affairs are not necessarily so constituted.

There is doubtless a genuine and important inquiry as to which combinations of words succeed and which fail to express real meaning, but such inquiry necessarily involves objective or ontologic reference. Thus it is meaningless to speak of drawing a perpendicular to two o'clock or sewing a button on an explosion. Why? Surely not because of the nature of the words as mere sounds or marks, but because of the nature of the objects denoted. Perpendicularity is a property of two lines in a certain relation to each other, and two o'clock is not a line at all but a point in time. The process of sewing a button requires, by definition, a physical body, which an event such as an explosion is not.

This brief indication of the condition for significant combinations of words fits in with our contention that words are incomplete symbols and verbal meanings are fragments of real meaning. Words have as much meaning as they do because they are defined by being used in sentences or their equivalents in gesture; and they can be combined only with such other fragments as are complementary parts of the originally defining wholes or unities. This becomes obvious when we deal with such combinations as round squares, or $2 \times 3 = 7$. In such cases, the *individual* words have verbal meaning, but analysis of the defining categories shows that no possible object can be denoted by these *combinations* of words. For such combinations involve self-contradiction or the mutual annihilation of parts which leaves us nothing. Whether certain combinations of words that seem intelligible by themselves do or do not have real meaning, is thus a significant inquiry, and not something always completely given by linguistic or syntactical form. Certainly no formula relating simply to the grammatical categories of the terms used, such as, for instance, noun, article, etc., can guarantee that a given combination will have meaning.

We may also add that sometimes we have the form but not the substance of intelligible statements. For example: " 'Twas brillig and the slithy toves did gyre and gimble," etc. Our analytic friends might well treat such combinations as propositional functions with euphonious sounds instead of the usual x's, y's, v's and z's. Thus we may say: It was a state of x, and the y kind of v's did perform the operation of z, etc. But however we put it, it is of the utmost importance to realize that propositional functions are not absolutely meaningless or devoid of all objective reference. Propositional functions are blanks which may be filled in with any one of a number of variables, and they may differ from each other as much as does an application blank for a position from the blank for an income tax return. Unless properly filled in they all remain blanks. Yet, one represents something common to all actual applications and the other something common to all proper income tax returns. We may say the same of all general statements. The law of multiple proportion, for instance, fails to identify or describe fully any specific chemical reaction. But it does indicate a repeatable pattern in nature. Such patterns or universal forms, though readily distinguishable, have no separate existence apart from particular embodiments. Such embodiment would make them particulars, as Aristotle pointed out long ago. But it is equally necessary to realize that specific objects or happenings do not exist apart from the forms or relations which determine them. The former would indeed be meaningless if they did not fit into certain categories which show them to be a part of an interrelated system—and this involves logical implication between the constituent parts.

To sum up: The attempt to make logic a matter of syntax of words assumes the primacy of words as essential to language. This obviously is false. We can convey information without the use of words in any way, for example, through the derisive laugh, or other forms of non-verbal expression. This may be illustrated by a story current at Harvard University. Students who regarded themselves as budding literary geniuses were in the habit of reading their papers to Professor C. One student made an appointment with Professor C to read to him an essay of which he was very proud. After a short while Professor C fell asleep. The student waited awhile, and then, seeing no sign of Professor C awakening, he put the paper into his pocket and started to walk out. Just then Professor C woke up. The student remarked, "I am sorry I did not have the benefit of your criticism." "Why," Professor C remarked, "is not sleeping a criticism?"

Even when words are used, they need not be significant in themselves. Such expressions as "pish posh," "tut tut" and the like, convey devastating criticism, or blank denial or contradiction. Indeed, it is hard to determine what is a word.[7] The grammar of most developed languages, such as English, Greek or Latin, is molded by non-logical considerations, which sometimes produce illogical results. The differences between grammar and logic are thus notorious, precisely because practical considerations often do violence to rules of grammar and syntax. A good example is the use of double negatives for the sake of emphasis. If the function of language is the communication of ideas, the double negative may produce an intended result without any uncertainty or indetermination.

[7] *Cf.* Professor Riess' more than one hundred definitions of what is a word.

There can be no one-to-one correspondence between words and what they denote, because in addition to the blanks or lazy or useless words described above, there are also in all languages pleonasms, homonyms, synonyms, and other verbal forms, producing ambiguities which in fact result in indeterminations as respects meaning or significance that can be obviated only by a knowledge of the subject matter or context. Sometimes the same word denotes opposites or contraries, such as "let" which denotes *allow* and *prevent;* or "fast" which denotes a kind of motion or fixed position, as in *stand fast.* Sometimes the word "or" stands for a relation of mutual exclusion and sometimes for a relation of identity, as in the case of words in apposition, as for example in the phrase, Queen Victoria *or* the sovereign of Great Britain. Indeed the prevalence of ambiguity in words is so notorious and has been remarked so often that it is amazing to find logicians who call themselves positivists blithely ignore that fact by refusing to take it into account in their uncritical acceptance of the dogma that syntax or some combination of words is always adequate to give us a definite meaning. Without a knowledge of the context any combination of words may fail to convey a determinate meaning.

Finally the sharp distinction that Carnap and others have tried to draw between expressions of emotion and factual statements seems to me invalid, since an expression of emotion may also contain, and frequently does, a statement of fact. Consider highly emotional expressions such as Jesus calling the Pharisees "vipers," "whited sepulchers," and the like. Can we say such expressions are entirely devoid of descriptive meaning? Similarly, imperatives also contain implicitly reference to the conditions under which they hold. Thus, we are in the habit of saying "If it please your Honor" but we may abbreviate it in other cases to "Please" and even omit the word "Please" and put the imperative simply: "Come" or "Do this."

4. *Implication*

We can now consider more closely the relation between real meanings and logical implication. The failure to distinguish clearly between formal and strictly logical implication, called by some logicians entailment, has led to the familiar paradoxes for which many cures have been offered. Peirce and others have called attention to the fact that purely logical implications have no significant alternatives. The assertion that x is a man implies x is mortal for all values of x is a formal assertion which may turn out to be false; but the assertion that there may be a fraction whose square is equal to 2, or Mill's assertion that in some other planet 2 + 3 might not equal 5, can be shown to be self-contradictory and thus meaningless as a whole, even though all the individual words of it seem significant because they are so in other sentences.

I think, however, that we can go further and insist that logical implication, strictly speaking, cannot be limited to propositions, if the latter are defined as material assertions that are always true or always false.

It was a great service to philosophy when Mr. Russell brought in the notion of material implication as a connecting relation between propositions. In doing this he showed clearly what Peirce and Bradley had indicated before him, namely, that logical principles such as that of the syllogism are the forms but not the premises of specific arguments. This cut the ground from all the attempts to *prove* the idealistic or spiritual view of the universe on strictly logical grounds. It also helped to show that we must not confuse the illative relation between what is asserted in two or more propositions, and the psychologic process of drawing inferences or perceiving that relation. Despite the great technical success, however, of the *Principia,* insufficient attention has been directed to the nature of strictly logical implication. Those who assume, as Russell does, the primacy of the propositional calculus, naturally think of implication as a relation between propositions. But if we realize that logical implication is independent of the truth or falsity of our hypotheses or premises, we can recognize, indeed as Russell himself does, that implication holds between propositional functions, e.g., x is a man implies that x is mortal. But if so, we may as well substitute terms or concepts for propositional functions and say that it is manhood which implies mortality. The sentence, "The Bolshevik Revolution took place in 1917," is generally taken as a proposition, and the phrase, "The Bolshevik Revolution of 1917," is taken as a term or concept. But is there any difference in their implications? It is sufficient to urge that if the distinction between a proposition and a concept is that the former must be true or false while the latter need not have that character, then deduction need not be limited to propositions, since expressions which are neither true nor false may have logical consequences. Truth and falsity apply to statements, but logical relations may be viewed ontologically as the invariants in the transformations of all possible objects. Logical implication is thus a necessary element of real meaning.

It has become the fashion to refer to logical propositions as tautologies, and there is no harm in using this term if by tautology we mean the assertion of exhaustive possibilities, such as "Madrid will be captured within a month or not." But any suggestion that logical statements are tautologies in the sense that they are devoid of any real or objective reference is altogether misleading. It is surely not insignificant to ask whether there may be constructed with ruler and compass a circle equal in area to a given square. This question involved long and arduous explorations, taking over 2,000 years. At no point can such inquiry be said to have been meaningless.

Furthermore, we have the historic fact that such inquiry (in the form of mathematics) has proved to be the most fruitful instrument in the exploration of nature. It is because strictly logical implications or, if you insist, tautologies, exhaust the field of possibility that they serve as the necessary though not sufficient condition for materially significant inquiries in the field of nature.

The great objection to the ontologic interpretation of logical relations has been the fear that if this be granted, we shall be opening the gates to the deduction of empirical or factual determinations from *a priori* considerations. This, however, is a *non sequitur*. From that which is common to all possible transformations of objects, nothing can be legitimately deduced as to that which characterizes some particular sub-class such as specific physical objects. It is only by recognizing the validity of universals, the implications between propositional functions, that we are enabled to avoid both the Charybdis of false rationalism which tries to deduce particular existences from pure universals, and the Scylla of blind positivism or empiricism which either denies genuine universals or by dubious induction tries to deduce them from mythically self-sufficient particulars.

What is it that we do when we apply mathematics to physics and deduce the logical consequences of such a statement as that of the law of gravitation? We disregard all the qualities which characterize specific physical entities and we show that if anything at all has certain traits, it will necessarily have certain others. The mathematical deduction proceeds by rules that are independent of the specific traits involved because they are applicable to all. The mathematics itself may then be regarded as a mere tautology but the meaning of any statement about physical nature would be incomplete without it. Logical implication is thus a necessary though not a sufficient condition of physical meaning.

Consider any statement about the nature of any object. What can we say about such a thing as a table without including its possible transformations? If, for instance, we say it has mass, we mean that certain things will happen under certain conditions. Thus, not only do all physical laws have reference to possibility but concrete statements about this or that physical object would be incomplete if we were to exclude reference to the possible. Facts are meaningless except as parts of a system; and science is possible and applicable to the actual world precisely because the actual world has repeatable patterns which can be abstracted and connected according to certain invariable relations. Real meaning, the nature of things, thus contains as one of its elements the logical invariants which hold of all possible transformations or of all possible objects.

When we are concerned with adding to our factual knowledge, we must be guided by a sense of what is necessary to complete the existing knowledge. No actual *material* knowledge can by itself determine the content of *additional* knowledge. The growth of such knowledge depends on new experience. Yet the directions of such growth, or the conditions which this new knowledge must meet in order to fit into what we already know, are determined by logical or mathematical considerations. What is called logical analysis is an exploration of the field of possibility. Such procedure may be called empirical in the sense that our possibilities are ways in which elements of the actual world can be arranged or transformed. Without such possible applications formal logic would be entirely meaningless. But it is rational in the sense that no new contingent facts can be the result of our logical analysis and that its procedure is not determined by any contingent fact. This is what is familiarly expressed by saying that there can be nothing in the concluson which was not contained, or, to be more exact, implied in the premises.

5. *Meaning and Verifiability*

What is verification? We speak of verifying a document, or reference, or quotation, when we want to make sure of its authenticity, without thereby raising the question of its meaning, although if the meaning is strange or unexpected we may resort to verification in this sense to allay our doubt. But an undiscriminating acceptance of empiricistic operationalism has identified the process of verification with the very existence of meaning, and led to the consequent assertion that metaphysical and ethical propositions are meaningless because unverifiable. A little reflection, however, shows that while the verification of any hypothesis does depend upon its having meaning (in the sense of logical consequences) it is quite arbitrary to assert that those consequences must be of the special kind involved in certain physical experiments. And it is clearly a metaphysical dogma of doubtful verifiability to assert that there is nothing in the world other than physical events or operations.

Carnap and others deny that any unverifiable proposition has meaning. This seems at the outset a violent *tour de force*. We do not ordinarily think the meaning of anything is identical with its verifiable consequences. All sorts of statements are ordinarily deemed significant or meaningful without it ever occurring to us to undertake their verification. Such is the case, for example, with ordinary suppositions, invitations, statements of problems, expressions of doubt, questions, statements of immediate perception, and statements of logical implication. Surely these and other types of intelligible statement have meaning without being verified. I say to someone, "Consider the case of a man drowning." This is an intelligible statement that does not call for verification.

Carnap, in general, identifies the verification of any proposition with its perceptible consequences, without, however, considering the exact nature of the perceptible, which, I take it, includes all objects of sensation,—the audible and the touchable, as well as the visual. Now, as James has shown in his *Principles of Psychology*, there is a difference between sensation and perception. Perception depends, among other things, on our attitudes towards a given problem which interests us and of which we are thinking.

Consider the proposition, "There are no snakes in Ireland." Surely that is intelligible and presumably has meaning. But how can we verify it? Suppose we traveled all over Ireland and saw no snakes. Surely that would not be an adequate verification. In fact, Carnap's assertion that unverified statements are meaningless is not itself verified. But that does not render it meaningless. Its significance lies in its use as a postulate of procedure, and this suggests a limitation of the narrow positivism or empiricism, in that it takes no account of any procedural postulates.

The process of verification involves two undertakings: first, we must deduce the consequences of the proposition to be verified; and second, we must examine these consequences to see whether they agree with or contradict the proposition in question. Now it is obvious that if a proposition were utterly meaningless, we should have no way of verifying it; in that case we should have no ground for discriminating between what does and what does not follow from the proposition. Utterly meaningless groups of words have no consequences, for only that which has meaning can have consequences. In point of fact, the process of verification is not at all simple. Take, for instance, the question whether there is or is not an ether, and whether it has or has not a "drag" on light rays. Some people did object that the issue was metaphysical, for they could not imagine any experimental consequences from an assumption of its existence, but the Michelson and Morley experiment devised a method of determining whether there is or is not such an influence on light rays.

Now the process of thinking out the possibility of such an experiment obviously depends on fortuitous circumstances. It requires ingenuity to think of such an arrangement as will decide the issue, and this requires knowledge of nature as well as the faculty of inventing new situations. Before such situations are invented, the original issue surely does not remain meaningless. Charles Peirce, a real philosopher who grew up in a laboratory and spent most of his life in experimental work, laid down the experimental or pragmatic theory of meaning as follows:

Consider what possible practical consequences the truth or falsity of the proposition in question may involve. These consequences constitute the meaning of the proposition in question. It will be seen that this test involves mental experiments, i.e., experiments in imagining possible consequences. By this test anything which has any conceivable consequences has meaning.

Consider the verification of purely mathematical propositions, such as a proposition about prime numbers. These propositions are surely verifiable, but not by any physical experiment. They require purely logical perceptions—that is, determinations of the question at issue whether certain propositions do or do not imply others. This is equally true of cases of direct sensory perception.

Carnap leaves out of account the fact that, as James pointed out, all perception depends on the problems that we set ourselves. And Poincaré pointed out the fallacy of the assumption that simple perception can produce absolute determination, since in all scientific work we have to correct our protocol readings by general theoretical considerations such as doctrines of probable error.

The fundamental error of the positivists arises from the fact that they view the world solely under the categories of determinate existence and non-existence, losing sight of the twilight zones in which most of our statements are made. They paint the world exclusively black or white to the utter neglect of the grays or other intermediate colors. I ask a man how soon will the war stop, and he replies with a shrug of his shoulders, which, though only a gesture, shows that he understands my question just as if he said, "I don't know." We are justified therefore in assuming that the question was understood—that it had meaning. Significant questions surely have meaning even before they are verified.

We may conclude that the realm of meaning is broader than the realm of propositions, that within this broader realm there are many instances of meaning without verification, and that even within the realm of propositions meaning cannot be limited to verification, for while the full meaning of any general theorem requires some exemplification, leading to verification, it is not true that without verification propositions are utterly meaningless.

Carnap's rejection of all metaphysical issues as unverifiable is too sweeping. Thus he rejects the issue of materialism as metaphysical. But materialism involves what is the essence of Carnap's physicalism, namely, the assumption that all phenomena in nature will show perceptible consequences. This I submit is the ordinary meaning of materialism. The issue is not completely settled or decided, because we cannot remove possible doubt as to whether consequences which are not *directly* perceptible do or do not take place.

Similar difficulties arise in characterizing as metaphysical, and therefore meaningless, the issue of spiritualism. Men of keen intelligence and extensive scientific experience have believed that the dead can communicate by words through intermediaries. If so, that would tend to prove the possibility of life beyond death. I do not argue for such a belief. I am merely suggesting that it is not meaningless.

Consider the issue between vitalism and mechanism. Surely this is a metaphysical issue which involves experimental consequences. Thus Driesch and others have argued that the organism has efficacy over and above the efficacy of any of its parts, and this is inconsistent with mechanism. But Jacques Loeb and others adduce a host of experimental consequences to show the validity of the mechanistic view. It is not necessary to decide the issue. It is enough to deny that it is meaningless. For the experimental consequences of one or the other view are legion.

We may extend this point of view to apply to other metaphysical issues, but that is hardly necessary. Such issues may be hard to settle definitively, because we do not have enough knowledge, and it may even be wise in that case not to bother about them. But it requires a strain on our credulity to believe that the issues which have agitated humanity so deeply throughout the ages are entirely devoid of meaning, and that men like Aristotle, Plato, Lotze, Leibniz, Kant, Spinoza and others, completely failed to realize this prior to its recent discovery by the logical positivists.

It may be as Kant, the greatest metaphysician of modern time, suggested, that we cannot have any knowledge beyond the realm of possible experience, but this leaves the question undetermined as to what are the limits or realms of possible experience. Surely it is not meet for a philosopher or any other serious thinker to quench all doubt by dogmatizing about that which we cannot know with certainty, though we have to risk our life, happiness and ultimate salvation on such guesses as we call faith.

According to the current popular view, a universal proposition is verified when its particular consequences are found to hold true in experience. Clearly, however, we can never examine *all* the temporal consequences of a genuinely universal hypothesis; and to argue that the truth of an assumption is proved when some of its consequences are found to be true is recognized in logic as an elementary fallacy. The popular view of verification, however, fails to distinguish it from confirmation; and we know that all sorts of faiths can find confirmation no matter what happens. What distinguishes complete scientific verification from such confirmation is not only the ability to predict what will happen but the ability to predict something inconsistent with any known alternative hypothesis. Now the elimination of such alternative hypotheses because disproved by some actual occurrence does not prove the one verified. Of course we may assume that all the possible hypotheses are before us. But such an assumption cannot be proved by any finite number of experiments or actual particular observations. Verification only shows an hypothesis to be better than its alternatives because it explains something that the others fail to do.

From this very brief analysis, it should be clear: (1) that it is impossible to restrict the meaning of a proposition to those consequences which turn out to be true in actuality—for we must be able to deduce consequences from false propositions in order to prove them false; and (2) it is precisely because natural science cannot prove an hypothesis to be absolutely true but only to be better than the others in the field, that it can make progress. Those who begin with the absolute truth cannot improve upon it.

But, we may ask, why is it that though crucial experiments are logically necessary for complete verification, the actual history of science shows relatively few instances of them? A number of different factors in the situation may well be invoked to explain this fact. But one is especially relevant to our present discussion, and that is that not all the hypotheses of science are such as can be refuted by a single experiment. No single throw of a penny can refute the assertion that the probability of a penny falling head is one-half. Indeed, there are many, who, like the astronomer, Proctor, hold that the assertion that the probability of a penny falling head is one-half will not be refuted by fifty consecutive occurrences of the penny falling tail. I do not think the latter view ultimately tenable. After all, it is experience which must decide what is the proper probability of a penny falling head. But it is the experience of a long run. Similarly, some methodological postulates may prove unwieldy and the assumptions underlying them untenable. But in the nature of the case it requires more than one experiment to demonstrate this.

If we thus distinguish between short range and long range verification, or if you like, between the direct and indirect form of it, we see that not only metaphysics, but history and many fields of natural science are not verifiable in the former way, but at best only in the latter way. Thus, we cannot today directly verify the existence of George Washington by any single experiment or observation which would conclusively disprove the possibility of his non-existence. Every bit of evidence in favor of the historicity of George Washington may be explained by some other hypothesis. The reason for maintaining the historical view is that its denial requires invoking all sorts of other assumptions that conflict or are inconsistent with so many of the assumptions that we cannot change. Without committing ourselves to the coherence theory of truth, we must recognize that the objects of true propositions are so connected as to form some sort of a world. Now metaphysics or general philosophy tries to formulate some world view using general principles to enable us to integrate all our knowledge. Its truth cannot therefore be conclusively tested by any one particular experiment, least of all by a purely physical one. Metaphysical propositions are perspectives. They determine the point of view from which all human experience or all our sciences and anticipations can be co-ordinated.

Certainly the man who believes that we have a Divine Father to look after us will see the particular events of human history in a different light than one who believes that the world is governed exclusively by physical forces. The two will certainly have different views as to the efficacy of prayer. The man who believes in the immortality of the soul regards life not only as continuing beyond death but also as less dependent upon bodily phenomena even during our earthly existence. One may take the agnostic position and say that the evidence in favor of the existence of God or the immortality of the soul is inadequate to prove anything. Or one may take the position that what little evidence we have points more to a negative than to a positive answer. But neither position will justify the assertion that the question as to the existence of God or the immortality of the soul is altogether meaningless.

Let me, in the interests of clarity, insist that I am not arguing for the traditional Theistic view of the world, nor am I denying the tenability of the physicalist point of view as an hypothesis. What I am doing is denying the validity of the pretended proof that all metaphysical propositions are essentially meaningless. Of course one can define meaning in such a way as to restrict it to purely physical phenomena in actuality, but no theorem as to objective existence can be disproved by a mere definition. We cannot disprove any doctrine as to ultimate existence without involving ourselves in some other doctrine of a metaphysical character, that is, of assumptions beyond the physically actual. For the assumption that there is nothing beyond the physical is in itself essentially metaphysical. It is a postulate, not an empirically known fact.

It is interesting to observe the logical analogy between the old idealistic argument that there cannot be an unknowable, and the positivistic argument that it is meaningless to speak of anything beyond the phenomenal. Both arguments seek to derive a highly debatable proposition from what is at best a bare identity. You can, of course, arbitrarily choose to define the words *being* and *knowable* as identical, but you cannot prove anything significant by that procedure. For the possibility and likelihood that there are existences which we do not know and may never know, cannot be thus eliminated. Similarly, you may identify the words *meaningful* and *physical* by an arbitrary definition or resolution. But the difference between what is ordinarily meant by *meaning* and by *physical existence* cannot be thereby wiped out. You may believe, as I do, that there is not enough evidence to prove the existence of disembodied spirits. But you cannot contend that the doctrine of physicalism is significant and yet maintain that its negation is meaningless.

Logical analysis, as practiced by Carnap, seems to be another term for what used to be called the fallacy of division. Thus Carnap tries to do away with the possibility of metaphysics or ethics by trying to show that they are neither empirical, nor *a priori*, nor tautologous, nor instances of logical analysis. In point of fact, even the wildest metaphysics contains many empirical elements as well as purely logical propositions.

If you break up any doctrinal whole into its constituent parts you cannot find the original whole in the separated parts. Metaphysics has always been a striving after ultimate synthesis, as opposed to what Berkeley called minute philosophies.

In what sense, if any, are metaphysical propositions verifiable? Assuming metaphysics to denote that which is beyond physics, as God, the immortal soul, etc., metaphysical propositions are obviously not verifiable in the way in which propositions about physics are verifiable. One may say that faith in God strengthens his life, and that is a postulate or resolution that takes the issue out of the field of ordinary proof or disproof. More disputable becomes the contention that not merely individuals, but masses of people who believe are better off or lead better lives than those who do not believe. The issue is inherently complicated because of the number of factors involved in deciding what masses do live better lives or to what that is due.

If metaphysics is taken in a wider sense of general philosophy or view of the world it is obviously not directly verifiable, since metaphysical theories do not attribute to objects specific traits that can be experimentally shown to be absent. When a metaphysic does make such assertions it is in fact making assertions about natural science. Facts are cross-sections or selections from the temporal stream; and not only metaphysics but all sciences are general perspectives from which facts are viewed, or schema into which they are arranged. Particular experiments telling us what happened at certain instants cannot exhaust the nature of things. There are always possibilities beyond what any number of past experiments can have exhausted. (*Speaking metaphysically or ontologically we should say that things are never complete but are always actualizing some of their possibilities and excluding others.*) Now, the world of knowledge cannot be restricted to isolated events, for all knowledge includes an immediate element and some constants in respect to which things change. The category of time, for instance, is formally complete. It can be so defined. But that which it includes cannot be completed at any one instant. All knowledge, therefore, assumes a formal element that is a necessary condition of all existence but not sufficient to determine the specific conditions of any actual experience. The ultimate individual, the ultimate particularity, is inexpressible in words that are repeatable. From the point of view of actuality there is no complete world, but the process of completion proceeds on certain lines or threads of identity which are the rules of logical consistency. And as this is a proposition often asserted by both positivists and idealists, we can agree with both, to the extent that they agree with each other.

To summarize our discussion of the last section: The realms of meaning and verification cannot be co-extensive. In order to be capable of verification any proposition must have sufficient meaning to enable us to deduce definite consequences and to devise decisive experiments which will enable us to tell definitely whether such consequences agree with or contradict any part of the proposition at issue. But the realm of meaning is wider than the realm of verification. Questions and postulates, for example, are significant or meaningful even before we have means of verifying them. Intelligence consists in doubting propositions, i.e., entertaining the possibility of their being either true or false. It may well be contended, of course, that we do not have the full meaning of any proposition before us until all the consequences can be determined, but that does not justify the contention that before such determination is made the proposition remains altogether meaningless. That would be equivalent to the process of climbing up a ladder and then denying its existence. (The identity of interrogatives or questions with what the logicians call "propositional functions" has been noted by Dr. Felix S. Cohen.[8])

The assertion that ethical propositions are meaningless is part of the traditional positivistic misconception of scientific method in supposing that it must be restricted to facts of actual existence. It misses the fact that logic, mathematics and all general theoretic sciences are directed to determine what is possible and what is impossible. No knowledge can exhaust the actual particular individual. In referring to any particular object or event science aims rather at getting at those abstract traits which it has in common with other objects and which are relevant for a given system. And every practical endeavor must likewise restrict itself to some abstract phase of the things we are concerned with. Every time we act rationally or deliberately we balance the possible consequences of different courses of action only one of which can be realized. Ethical judgments are concerned with what men generally should do if they wish to be wise or completely rational in their choices. And though its elaboration is beset with almost insuperable difficulties there is no conclusive reason why ethics may not follow the ideal of rigorous scientific method—systematizing not only judgments of existence but also judgments as to what is desirable if certain ends are to be attained.[9]

8 "What is a Question?" 39 *Monist* (1929), p. 350.
9 The positivistic argument against the possibility of ethical science is treated in somewhat greater detail in chapter 8, *Values, Norms and Science, infra.*

I V

Concepts and Twilight Zones [1]

The three main theses which I wish to support are:

I. That concepts are signs, generally verbal, pointing to in-variant relations or transformations in the natural world (as against the classical doctrine that they are always generic mental images).

II. That, though these invariant elements make the definite-ness of science, there are elements of indetermination in the denotation of concepts, regions in which opposite statements are equally true.

III. That the relative extent of illumined focal region and twilight or penumbral zone varies with different concepts, and that the recognition of such variation provides important help in dealing with various logical and metaphysical problems, in the classification of intellectual temperaments, and in practical affairs.

1. *Concepts and Signs*

According to the classical doctrine adhered to in our text-books on logic, psychology, and education, concepts are general images abstracted from percepts. We begin our mental life with percepts of this or that table, this or that metal, etc. In the process of comparison the features in which the different tables

1 The substance of this chapter was published in *The Journal of Philoso-phy*, vol. 24 (1927), p. 673.

or metals vary, drop out, and the common elements are thus abstracted from the particular instances and are formed into generalized pictures of all the tables or metals we have seen. The essence of conceptualism is that this composite picture exists in the mind only and that only the particular tables or metals really exist in nature.

Against this view the following points may fairly be made:

1. *Concepts are not general images*

(*a*) Against the possibility of *general* "ideas" (as images or pictures), the argument of Berkeley seems to me still valid. A general picture of every possible triangle could itself be neither equilateral nor isosceles, nor scalene, and yet there cannot be a triangle that does not fall into one of these categories. The same objection can be repeated against the "idea" of an animal that is not vertebrate or invertebrate, of a metal that has not the color or either iron or mercury, gold or silver, etc. There may be "ideas" or images so blurred and vague that they cannot be said to be definitely particular, but such "ideas" are certainly not what we refer to when we speak of the definite concepts of the exact sciences.

(*b*) Recent psychology seems to justify the doubt, expressed long ago by Burke, as to whether people who understand what is meant by *right, liberty, justice,* etc., have any corresponding images other than the words or sounds, and whether even more concrete concepts universally arouse any other images in the course of ordinary rapid conversation or reading.

(*c*) In any case, it seems clear that the determination of the *meaning* of concepts like ratio, energy, gravitation, normal distribution, etc., is entirely independent of the psychologic question as to what images, if any, are in our minds when we think of these objects, just as the question concerning the physical structure of objects is independent of that relating to the character of our retinal images.

2. *Concepts not mere sums of abstract characteristics.*

(*a*) The classical doctrine views all concepts as formed by abstracting the marks or characteristics common to all instances to which the concept applies. The mechanical view of these marks as external to each other leads to a mechanical interpretation of the "law" of the inverse proportion between the extension and intension, as if it were universally true that the wider our generalization, the less significance it can carry. If this were always true, knowledge of the general could never give us increased insight into particulars: we could never understand osmosis the better for knowing the nature of pressure, nor human physiology the better because of our knowledge of vertebrate physiology, nor English grammar and law because of the study of general grammar and jurisprudence. The classical notion that every concept is composed of a definite number of distinct characteristics leads consistently to the old rationalistic distinction between analytic and synthetic judgments (*cf.* Kant's Introduction to the *Critique of Pure Reason*). This theory breaks down in its account of the necessary and yet fruitful character of deduction, a breakdown which is not relieved by Kant's invention of *a priori* intuitions of time and space, which turn out to be unverifiable and entirely unnecessary for actual mathematical procedure.

(*b*) Against the classical doctrine we may also urge the existence of concepts which have only one object, e.g., the physical world, the science of arithmetic, absolute zero, Buddhism, or the history of mankind. Whether or not we accept Russell's theory that a relation such as *difference* has no instances and that whenever two things differ, there we have the same relation of difference, there can be no doubt that concepts such as *difference* denote relations that cannot be reduced to properties of things, like their colors and weights.

3. *Concepts concerned with relations or transformations*

Any survey of the actual concepts of modern science will show that they are all predominantly concerned with relations, operations, or transformations rather than with classes or kinds of things and their qualities. The emphasis of classical logic on genus and species was probably due to the fact that Aristotle's principal scientific preoccupation was with classificatory zoology and botany and that British empiricists like Mill had no wider range of primary scientific interests. In any case, it is clear that classification is but a subordinate feature of modern science, which is dominated by experimental statistical and mathematical considerations. Hence modern logic, to the extent that it has actually come into contact with modern science (as it has in mathematical logic), has been forced to give up the universality, or at least the primacy, of the old analysis of everything into substance and attribute. To view number, for instance, as a quality of things leads to insuperable difficulties when we come to deal with complex numbers or real numbers like the square root of two, difficulties which are avoided when we recognize that even integral numbers are operations, viz., the correlation of all similar groups or aggregates. If we ask what is common to all the letters of the alphabet we can hardly expect a significant answer unless we start with the concept of the alphabet and recognize a certain identity of function in all the letters. The relational or operational logic has thus proved to be far wider and more serviceable than the older classificatory logic. All the truth of the latter can be maintained in the former by interpreting concepts of genus and species in terms of functions with variable terms. Thus a table is anything which serves a certain purpose in certain ways; an animal is not a composite picture or a bundle of properties common to cow and starfish, but anything which behaves in certain ways, etc.

4. *The meaning of concepts*

Stated positively: *Concepts are signs (mainly audible or visible words and symbols) pointing to invariant relations,* i.e., relations which remain identical despite the variations of the material in which they are embodied. Significant concepts, therefore, enable us to arrange in order and hold together diverse phenomena, because of some real unity of process or relation which constitutes an element of identity between them. As our knowledge develops and our concepts become more comprehensive they do not become thinner or less significant. On the contrary, they become more significant because, as they are cleared of accidental associations, they point to relations and operations which really unify diverse phenomena and reveal unexpected characteristics. Thus the term "mass" begins in mechanics by pointing to the quality of resistance to touch, which varies in complex ways; when, however, it is developed and defined more abstractly as a ratio between forces and accelerations, we are enabled to perceive an element identical in mechanical inertia as well as in light, electricity, and gravitation. That which thus enables us to correlate diverse phenomena also enables us to understand each the better. The concept "French" is not necessarily thinner or less significant than that of "Parisian." The meaning of the term "European" does not involve dropping of all differences between French and German, but, on the contrary, makes this difference significant by deriving it from the operation of a common nature working under different conditions—geographic, political, etc. Deduction is thus fruitful to the extent that we start from real unitary or universal transformations that retain their character when applied to all sorts of diverse material or when joined to all sorts of subsidiary transformations.

This view also enables us to cut the ground of the skeptical arguments of Bergson and James that concepts are static and fixed and cannot grasp the nature of reality which is ever changing or growing. It is rather the ordinary percepts of tables, metals, animals, etc., which represent the more or less habitual cross-sections of the changing world. But the genuine concepts of science, especially the mathematical ones, denote the relations or transformations that are the clues to the understanding of the various changes about us. This they do by making us see the pattern of these changes and the invariant characteristics which make things keep their identity throughout the change. We thus explain both the fact of change and the reason why things seem to have the relatively fixed nature which they do show.

The new logic does not deny the categories of substance, things, and qualities, but it provides greater scientific insight by viewing things not merely as bearers of qualities, but more significantly as also centers for changing relations and capacities.

5. *The objective theory of meaning*

According to the prevailing view, the relation of meaning which holds between signs and the objects to which they point is in the mind only. This is a truism if we hold that both signs and that which they denote are equally mental. But in this case the term "mental" denotes everything and does not exclude anything, and thus becomes too wide to characterize the specific nature of *meaning*. If, however, we view mind as something to which there is an external nature, the relation of meaning cannot be merely mental, but must in some way exist or subsist in the same external nature in which we find the physical sign and the terms between which it holds. This does not deny the existence of consciousness in organisms to which certain signs become significant because of certain physical happenings. We may even admit the existence of private and purely conventional signs (artificial memoranda, ciphers, etc.), but the concepts of science clearly presuppose a common natural world in which communication may be established by means of the identity of relations which hold between certain conventional and natural entities. That conventional language has a natural basis becomes clear when we examine the process of establishing a language between those who had no communication before, e.g., Columbus and the West Indians, or a child and his parents.

2. *Twilight Zones*

It is commonly recognized that scientific concepts introduce definiteness and precision into our view of the world. This recognition is generally associated with the view that the world of nature is always definite and that only our ideas of it are more or less indefinite. It seems to me that there is a sense in which there are also regions of indetermination in the natural world itself. At any rate the objective denotation of our concepts may be of different degrees of definiteness.

Definiteness is generally produced by sharp antitheses and

rigorous dichotomous divisions based on the logical principles of contradiction and excluded middle. These principles, our logic books warn us, do not mean that everything is either white or black, soft or hard, warm or cold, virtuous or sinful. For there may be things that belong to neither alternatives. Velocities are neither white nor black, virtues are not literally soft or hard, etc. But our logic books do not warn us against the much more serious common error of denying that things can be both white and black, soft and hard, warm and cold, alive and dead, visible and invisible, though, of course, not in the same relation or respect. It is the neglect of this needed warning that makes the term *logical* frequently used as a term of deserved reproach. We may be most vigorous anti-Hegelians and realize the intellectual suicide involved in denying or even softening the distinction between opposites. Yet we must grant that of things in transition there are times when opposite predicates are equally true. We cannot, in fact, draw an absolutely sharp dividing line between day and night, or say when a man ceases to be alive and becomes dead. No distinction seems sharper than that between the visible and the invisible. Yet actually there is no sharp line dividing what we see from what we do not see. If we disregard the rapid mobility of our eyes, our field of vision at any moment is neither finite nor infinite, but tapers off from the illumined focal regions of attention to the region of the invisible.

How do we reconcile the absoluteness of logical distinctions with the actual coexistence of opposites in these twilight zones?

The answer is that the laws of logic apply to the realm of essence, i.e., to natural existences only in so far as they are determinate. If nature means the realm of the determinate, then obviously all the indetermination exists in another realm which we may call *maya, mind,* or something else and which will necessarily have to be viewed as non-natural. If, however, nature includes both determination and indetermination, our empirical view of things can be explained as well as the growth of scientific or mathematical knowledge. On the nominalistic theory that concepts are mere words or sounds, or on the conceptualist theory that they are something in the mind only, nature is entirely alogical and there can be no valid explanation of why nature should conform to the laws of the logical operations of a mind to which it is external. But according to the realistic theory nature *is* determined by operations which our concepts denote, and obeys the laws of logic to the extent that it is so determined. There is, however, nothing in logic or nature to prevent the existence of complexes in which contrary tendencies are conjoined. The law of contradiction is that nothing can be both *a* and not-*a in the same relation.* But physical entities or complexes of relations admit and often demand contrary determinations within them. Of any given individual it may be true to say that he is generous and not generous at the same time. The truth of both of these statements becomes clear and determinate if we draw a distinction and say he is generous to his family and in public charities, but ungenerous to his employees and economic competitors. A body cannot be moving north and south at the same time, but it may be pulled both north and south, and its actual path may be the resultant of the two opposite poles. The law of contradiction does not bar the presence of contrary determinations in the same entity, but only requires as a postulate the existence of a distinction of aspects or relations in which the contraries hold.

The last example suggests that to make logic applicable to empirical issues, we must employ the principle of polarity. By this I mean that the empirical facts are generally resultants of opposing and yet inseparable tendencies like the north and south poles. We must, therefore, be on our guard against the universal tendency to simplify situations and to analyze them in terms of only one of such contrary tendencies. This principle of polarity is a maxim of intellectual search, like the principle of causality, against the abuse of which it may serve as a help. If the principle of causality makes us search for operating causes, the principle of polarity makes us search for that which prevents them from producing greater effects than they do. In physical science the principle of polarity would thus be represented by the principle of action and reaction, and the principle that wherever there are forces there must be resistance. In biology it has been expressed by Huxley, in the aphorism that protoplasm manages to live only by continually dying. This finds its ethical analogue in the mutual dependence of the concepts of self-sacrifice and self-realization. Philosophically it may be generalized as the principle, not of the identity, but of the necessary copresence and mutual dependence of opposite determinations. It warns us against the greatest bane of philosophizing, to wit: the easy artificial dilemma between unity and plurality, rest and motion, substance and function, actual and ideal, etc. Professor Felix Adler has used the figure of the scissors to denote the fact that the mind never operates effectively except by using both unity and plurality like the two blades which move in opposite directions. Professor Marshall, in his *Principles of Economics,* has used the same figure to denote the mutual dependence of the economic factors of supply and demand. At other times the action of our jaws in mastication, or the necessity of applying a brake when you are going down hill, have appealed to me as representative figures of what I have in mind. Physical science employs this principle to eliminate the vagueness and indetermination of popular discussion in which opposite concepts, like good and bad, hot and cold, large and small, remote and near, can be applied to the same thing. Such vagueness is eliminated by substituting concepts of numbers and measures, which enable us to pass from relatively indeterminate issues as to whether our object is large or small, hot or cold, to the more definite issue, how many yards, how many degrees of temperature, etc. Similar progress might be made in philosophy if we recognized the indeterminateness of certain issues as to whether certain things exist or not, by asking, exist how or in what sense.

From the point of view of the principle of polarity, twilight zones are regions about the point of equilibrium of opposite tendencies. For this reason all concepts which swallow up their own negatives, like the concepts of reality, existence, experience, the universe, etc., are essentially indefinite in meaning.

We conclude, then, that, while in the realm of formal or strictly logical concepts there can be no twilight zones, such zones are always present in the realm of psychical and physical existence. Whatever difficulties or possible contradictions may be found in the foregoing account, the facts seem certain that all words or combinations of words which do not point either to an inarticulate here and now or to purely logical relations do point to a universe in which there are elements of indetermination, or at least of different degrees of definiteness.

3. *Applications*

That the relative extent of twilight zone and focal illumination varies with different concepts can be made evident if we barely juxtapose concepts like *a long distance, a day's journey,* and *thirty-five miles* or a *good machine* and one that is *seventy per cent. efficient,* or an unpopular magistrate and one that has a majority against him. This recognition of the diversity in the extent of the twilight zone can be applied in logic, metaphysics, psychology, physics, economics, politics, art, social life, and religion.

1. *Formal Logic.* (*a*) In the doctrine of definition our analysis helps us to understand the greater definiteness of groups of words giving the meaning of a single one, e.g., defining the Nordic type by the color of eyes, hair, etc. It also enables us to see the importance of using in our definition terms with smaller penumbras than the terms defined.

(*b*) In the doctrine of division and all that depends upon it we are warned against the widespread fallacy of supposing that any classification of natural objects can have the absolute rigor of logical division. The twilight zones between the classes of plants and animals, between vertebrates and invertebrates, need not disturb the biologist whose principles of division are based on concepts of wide and significant application. For practical purposes also we must adopt classifications that have even larger overlapping regions, for example, the sane and the insane, the normal and the abnormal, the well and the sick. It would be the height of unwisdom to refuse to adopt a useful classification because it breaks down in a practically negligible number of cases. But the confusion between the practicality of empirical classifications (to be tested by their applicability) and the absoluteness of division based on logical principles, is perhaps the most fruitful source of philosophic error. No other group of intellectual workers is so addicted to the use of sharp alternatives and to the easy assumption that things *must* be in one of the compartments we provide for them *a priori*. There is reason to suppose that most philosophical errors (except when dealing with purely logical concepts) are downright fallacies; and metaphysical certainty as to matters of fact is the result of ignorance of anything to contradict our assertion.

2. *Metaphysics*. Our analysis enables us not only to avoid nominalism and conceptualism, but also to see the inadequacy of two types of realism, to wit: the atomic and the organic.

By the atomic type I mean that which tends to think of the world as devoid of genuine transitional or twilight zones. It thus includes such philosophies as the Kantian, so far as the latter is addicted to absolute metaphysical distinctions all in black and white without any grays, perhapses, or probabilities. This type of thought is strong in examining the logical characteristics of diverse concepts; but it generally tends to overlook the variation of their objects and the dependence of such variations upon the universe in which they occur. The great philosophic weakness is its uncritical reliance on sharp dilemmas between the ideal and the real, the material and the spiritual, the static and the dynamic, the mechanical and the organic, the old and the new, the active and the contemplative, etc. Philosophers who regard their point of view as functional, dynamic, organic, and new, may resent their metaphysics being placed in the category of the atomic. Yet to the extent that their arguments rest on sharp alternatives between such concepts as substance and function, their roots are in the soil of atomism.

By the organic type of metaphysics I mean the tendency which disparages sharp antithesis and distinctions, and thus confuses all things into one gray mixture. (Neo-Hegelians, like Bosanquet, seem to me to be typical of this tendency.) It has its logical roots in the view which regards the nature of concepts as determined by the contexts in which they occur, and thus tends to arrive at the logical conclusion that it is the whole universe that is the real subject of every significant proposition. It thus tends to call attention to the complexity of things and to avoid superficial clarity. But it systematically undervalues the importance of abstractions and does scant justice to the relative independence of the various parts of the world. The absolute totality of things is too indefinite (as well as the object of too much ignorance) to explain anything in it.

3. *The Rationalistic and Mystic Types of Intellect.* This new analysis of atomic and organic metaphysics suggests the possibility of viewing thinkers as predominantly either rationalistic or mystic. The rationalists are those who love sharp distinctions, clear subdivisions of structure, and hate blurred outlines and overlapping areas. They regard themselves as the clear-minded, opposed to the muddy-minded mystics. But the mystic is conscious of the wealth of being and possible experience, not yet made definite, which perhaps never can be made definite.

Your symbols, he says to the rationalist, are clear and stand next to each other in definite lines; but that to which they point is wider and deeper. The clearness and definiteness are dearly purchased at the price of comprehensive and deep sensibility. Clarity may be the result of superficiality, concentration and willful narrowness.

One might be tempted to say, with Levy-Brühl, that the mystic type is more primitive, that the vague consciousness is more primitively substantial and that distinctions are the result of intellectual experience. A great deal of evidence can be given for this view, to wit: primitive religious experience, the reliance on the mutterings of frenzied priestesses, and the belief that the demented are possessed of superhuman wisdom. But it should also be noted that children and the intellectually undeveloped are extreme rationalists. They divide all things into the good and the bad. In their popular novels and melodramas as well as in their fairy tales all characters are black or white, heroes or villains. Perhaps it would be better to say that what is primitive is the aversion for distinctions, or fine discriminations. The unreflecting man dislikes to be asked what he means by good or bad, etc. And he is irritated if in answer to his questions whether you believe in God you tell him that that depends on his definition of God. Thus melodrama and fairy tales are rationalistic in the sharp distinctions which they draw between the good and the bad characters, but mystical in their refusal to subdivide and introduce many subtypes. All heroes, villains, princes, and princesses are of the same mold.

4. *Practical Applications.* (*a*) If we revert to our example of the relative extent of twilight zone in the concepts of *long distance, a day's journey,* and *thirty-five miles,* we can make clear to ourselves the importance of measurement. It eliminates the vagueness of individual estimates by correlating them with phenomena of small variability, such as the length of the day, the length of rods and chains, etc.

(*b*) The same extraordinary usefulness of mathematical concepts in eliminating the waste of indetermination, shows itself also in the organization of our social institutions. In politics we have on the one hand the essentially twilight concepts of social welfare, the good of the state, national honor, etc., and on the other hand the concepts of majority rule, proportional representation, taxation based on percentage of income, etc. Passing over the whole field of economics where the application of our doctrine is too obvious, it is well to note how the life of legal institutions which aim to delimit human interests and to avoid conflicts, depends on the effort to find concepts with smaller twilight zones to replace those with very large ones. One illustration may suggest many others. It is generally recognized that some people are not competent to conduct their own affairs. The efficiency of the law depends on finding concepts more definite than the practically vague one of incompetency. Thus the law has to invent machinery for determining legal insanity, and it fixes the age of discretion at twenty-one (for most civil purposes). When does a man become twenty-one years of age? To remove some actual indefiniteness in people's answers to this question the law has had to invent a special rule to determine just when a man becomes twenty-one. In these as other matters, such as when the day ends and night begins, the law attains definiteness by utilizing the results of mathematical astronomy. In general, in law as in politics and economics, the value of substituting definite knowledge for vague beliefs is obvious. The law, therefore, endeavors to delimit the boundaries of conflicting interests as sharply as the facts will allow. But here as elsewhere the drawing of sharp lines has its dangers, and every legal system does violence to the finer social susceptibilities by its ignoring of individual differences. Hard and fast rules also depress social initiative and make legalism a curse. Hence the best legal minds always recognize the necessity of equity or *epieike* which comes into play with the sense of justice of the individual judge.

In social life, art, and religion, rules are as necessary as elsewhere for security and for economizing the fitful tides of life and inspiration, but the danger of rigid rules is clearest in these fields. And human wisdom consists in recognizing both the supreme claim of rational effort and its pathetic inadequacy.

V

On the Logic of Fiction [1]

The traditional Aristotelian logic is essentially the logic of classes of existences or facts. While the fundamental principles of this logic can never, I believe, be shown to be false—and in that sense there cannot be a strictly non-Aristotelian logic—it has in modern times been shown to be of limited applicability. In the first place, being inspired by classificatory zoology as the ideal science, it cannot come as close to the actual methods of the mathematical and dynamic sciences as does the more modern logic of De Morgan, Boole, Peirce, Peano, Frege, Russell and Whitehead. To attain the results of the latter by syllogistic methods would be, if not impossible, so cumbrous as to be devoid of any utility. In the second place, the Aristotelian logic, being fundamentally based on the primacy of individual or particular existence, inevitably tends to belittle the metaphysical status of universals, relations, or processes. This tends to create an initial positivistic bias against mathematical or theoretic science, and against normative sciences such as ethics or esthetics. For these sciences deal primarily not with existing things or facts, but with laws or ideals of what must be or should be, and they could have no right to the claim of being sciences if it were true that logically organized science can deal only with what factually is. However, as it is undoubtedly true that all sciences depend on theoretic or mathematical methods, and that all judgments on

1 The substance of this chapter was published in *The Journal of Philosophy*, vol. 20 (1923), p. 477.

human relations involve the normative standpoint of valuation, it becomes clear that the logic of *existences* depends upon the logic of *validity*. Moreover, since all developed sciences depend upon the process of comparing the consequences of rival hypotheses, it follows that correct or valid consequences can also be drawn from false hypotheses. The realm of valid logical inference is, therefore, wider than the realm of factual existence. The logic of fiction belongs to this realm of non-factual logic.

Aristotle himself in a famous passage in his *Poetics* clearly rejected the positivistic implication of his logic, by asserting that poetry is truer and more earnest than history (or factual investigation). This dictum, which is generally felt to contain a profound truth, cannot be justified on the Aristotelian logic which divides all propositions so sharply into the existentially true and false as to leave no room for poetry or fiction except in the realm of the false. In the attempt to explore the realm of non-factual validity, it is hoped that the truth of this famous dictum will become clearer.

1. *The Logic of Metaphors—Figurative Truth*

To appreciate the intellectual or scientific function of metaphors the reader had better begin with an experiment. Let him pick out a page or two of philosophic prose in any classical treatise or modern discussion. Let him read this extract carefully and mark the number of passages in which the meaning is suggested metaphorically rather than literally. Let him then read the passage a second time and reflect how many of the passages first taken as literal truths are really metaphors to which we have become accustomed. I mean such expressions as "the root of the problem," "the progress of thought," "the higher life," "falling into error," "mental gymnastics," and the like. Indeed, whenever we speak of the mind doing anything, collecting its data, perceiving the external world, and the like, we are using the metaphor of reification, just as we use the metaphor of personification whenever we speak of bodies attracting and repelling each other. The third stage of the experiment is to try to rewrite the passage in strictly literal terms without any metaphors at all. I believe that the result of such experiment will confirm the conclusion that to eliminate all metaphors is impossible. This is especially clear when we try to express general considerations of a novel or unfamiliar character. For, how can we apprehend new relations except by viewing them under old categories? At any rate, the experiment will make more plausible the view that metaphors are not merely artificial devices for making discourse more vivid and poetical, but are also necessary for the apprehension and communication of new ideas. This is confirmed by the history of language and of early poetry as well as by the general results of modern psychology.

The prevailing view since Aristotle's *Rhetoric* regards every metaphor as an analogy in which the words of comparison, *like* or *as,* etc., are omitted. This presupposes that the recognition of the literal truth precedes the metaphor, which is thus always a conscious transference of the properties of one thing to another. But history shows that metaphors are generally older than expressed analogies. If intelligence grows from the vague and confused to the more definite by the process of discrimination, we may well expect that the motion common to animate and inanimate beings should impress us even before we have made a clear distinction between these two kinds of being. Thus it is not necessary to suppose that the child that kicks the chair against which it has stumbled personifies the chair by the process of analogy. The reaction is clearly one arising on the undifferentiated level.

Metaphors may thus be viewed as expressing the vague and confused but primal perception of identity which subsequent processes of discrimination transform into the clear assertion of an identity or common element (or relation) which the two different things possess. This helps us to explain the proper function of metaphors in science as well as in religion and art, and cautions us against fallacious arguments for or against views expressed in metaphorical language.

The Function of Metaphors in Science. If it is true that the first perceptions of the new in experience tend to assume metaphoric expression, metaphors must play a large part in opening up new fields of science. In its search for the truth science must formulate some anticipation of what it expects to find. Such anticipation is clearly not fictional even if it turns out to be false, provided it has been held as an hypothesis to be tested. In trying to visualize the unknown, the imagination must clothe it with attributes analogous to the known. That this is actually the case a few examples will indicate:

(a) In the science of electricity the notion of an electric fluid was really never more than a metaphor. But it suggested many fruitful analogies, such as differences of level, direction of flow, etc. Faraday's suggestion of lines or tubes of force may have been taken by many in a more or less literal sense, but the present electron theory shows that it was a metaphor, justified in its day by the fruitful analogies to which it led.

(b) In psychology the metaphor of "states of mind" led to analogies such as the association of ideas, which laid the beginning of modern psychology. James' metaphor of "stream of consciousness" has led to an emphasis on the more continuous aspects of mental life. His analogy between habit and the way paper creased on a given line will always fold more readily on that line, illustrates the power as well as the snares of metaphoric illumination in science.

(c) In metaphysics the idea that the world is a machine working according to mechanical laws, or that it is an organism developing according to a fixed plan, is clearly metaphoric. So is the analysis of everything into substance and inherent qualities, analogous to a man and his possessions or clothes. It is well known that the categories of cause, force, law, are anthropomorphic in origin and were thus originally metaphors.

Each of these, like the various mechanical models of ether or of various unknown physical processes, suggests verifiable analogies and thus directs research. If these directions turn out false, our analogy has acted like a false hypothesis. But the term *fiction* may be applied to certain imaginary and unverifiable entities that vivify our conceptions but are strictly irrelevant to the truth or falsity of our conclusions. Thus Helmholz's and Poincaré's one- and two-dimensional beings, Maxwell's "sorting demon," and similar entities in social science, are really metaphors to express abstract relations. Where one of the figures is used any one of an infinity of others could be substituted, just as, according to Poincaré's proof, wherever a mechanical model is used an infinity of others is possible. When, therefore, these metaphors are taken literally we have the myths of which popular science is full.

It must be recognized, however, that metaphors are not always invented to vivify discourse. They are often the way in which creative minds perceive things, so that the explicit recognition that we are dealing with an analogy rather than a real identity comes later as a result of further reflection or analysis. Though undiscriminating, such primitive perception is likely to be most vivid and its apt expression becomes current coin, so that it becomes difficult if not impossible to distinguish between metaphor and literal truth.

As the essence of science is the search for truth, it seeks to eliminate these irrelevant fictions through the use of technical terms or symbols that denote the abstract relations studied and nothing else. But as no human terms can adequately express (though they can point to or adumbrate) the unknown, science is engaged in an endless process of self-correction and revision of its language. Such a process is irksome to popular discourse and to the social sciences to the extent that they depend on the latter. Hence our language becomes a prolific source of mythology.

2. *Practical Value of Metaphors.* The fact that metaphors express the primal perception of things with something of its undifferentiated atmosphere gives these metaphors an emotional power which more elaborate and accurate statements do not have. This is perhaps best seen in the profoundly simple metaphors of the New Testament. "Feed my sheep" is more potent than "teach my doctrine" because it carries with it the atmos-

phere of suggestion which those genuinely moved to preaching feel before they can formulate it—the tender sympathy to the helpless, the distress of the spiritually hungry, shown especially in the tense, open-mouthed faces of an oriental audience, etc. The same is true of the simile "sowing the seed of truth," or St. Paul's metaphor of preaching as "edification," of the righteous life as "girding on the armor of light," "garrisoning or fortifying the heart." Goethe's metaphor "Gray is all theory" is a vivid expression of what it would require considerable reflection to formulate in purely literal terms. So in practical affairs, the personifying of cities or nations, the likening of the state to a ship ("don't rock the boat"), or of changes of attitude to "the swing of the pendulum," contains a potency which literal statements do not have.

3. *Fallacies.* Various fallacies result from the inadequate realization of the metaphoric character of many propositions. Locke's metaphor of the mind as a *tabula rasa* illustrates the general principle. It is obviously fallacious to argue against this, as some have done, that the mind is neither a *tabula* nor *rasa* and that nothing literally makes impressions on the mind, as a stylus on a wax tablet. If there is any respect in which the metaphor can be transformed into a true analogy all these arguments are futile. Obviously there are many such analogies: e.g., the greater vividness of the first impressions, or the greater receptivity of the original state. But it is obvious, also, that this metaphor leads to many false analogies, e.g., the conception of the mind as purely passive or receptive in sensation.

Similar considerations hold with respect to such metaphors as social organism, social forces, or the external world.

This point of view will prevent us from misunderstanding the influence of symbols, and from committing the fallacy involved in the ordinary contemptuous reference to fetishism. The Hebrews could not understand the psychology of Greek and Roman "idol" worshipers, simply because the Greek idols were not to the Hebrews familiar symbols carrying with them vital penumbras of meaning. The Hebrews themselves, of course, had their own symbolic objects, the stones in the ark of the covenant, the scroll of the law (in later times), etc. That a sharp distinction between any symbolic object and that which it symbolizes is not primary, is illustrated by a debate in our own House of Representatives. Upon being pressed as to his attitude to the country's flag, the Socialist Congressman replied that he regarded the flag as but the symbol of the life of the people and that he respected the people, etc. The distinction was entirely too subtle for a Democratic congressman from Texas, who kept on pressing Congressman London as to his attitude to the flag itself.

2. *Ceremonial Expressions*

1. *Literal and Conventional Meanings.* Though it cannot be denied that every proposition is either true or false, a great many fallacies result if we ignore conventional meaning. Thus medieval poetry is full of allusions to the fragrance of the daisy. But it would be erroneous to argue that Chaucer did not know that actual daisies have no scent. The expression is conventional, like *"my dear sir,"* or *"your humble servant will meet you on the field of honor."*

It is well known that just as men and women will not wear the same clothes on radically different occasions, they will not use the same modes of expression. We do not use precisely the same language in public address as in private conversation, in writing as in speech, in poetry as in prose. This is generally recognized, but its logical significance has not been sufficiently attended to. Thus the common courtesy which refers to persons or groups by the characteristics which they would like or ought to have, is fruitful of much intellectual confusion. Many, for example, have built elaborate arguments on the assumption that Christian nations are monogamous and that Mohammedans are polygamous, though it is extremely doubtful whether in point of fact there is any great actual difference other than the question of legal status. This is true of the old arguments from the maxim that the king could do no wrong, or the modern ones that in a democratic

country the law is the will of the people, that law leaves everyone free, that it protects the poor equally as well as the rich, etc.
These statements are in a sense true, but are dubious on the
ordinary factual level. Sometimes it is, of course, doubtful
whether expressions are or are not intended to be taken literally,
e.g., when the Japanese admiral attributes a victory to the virtue
of the emperor, or when army bulletins attribute victories to
"the will of God and the courage of our troops."

The role of ceremonial expressions in the outer forms of make-
believe is as important in social life generally as in the games of
children and of primitive man. The social life of a country like
England may be viewed as a game that requires among other
things that the people should speak of His Majesty's army, navy,
or treasury (though the debt is national), and that the actual
leaders of the government should speak of "advising" the king
where the latter has practically no choice but to obey.

2. *Euphemisms.* Ceremonial expressions are often attacked as
conventional lies when they are intended not to deceive but to
express the truth euphemistically. Courtesy or politeness demands the elimination not necessarily of the truth, but of certain
unpleasant expressions that are for some reason or other taboo.
This is readily explained by the fact that words have emotional
effects on their own account. Thus it is permissible to refer to a
female (or lady) dog, but bad taste to use the single-syllabled
word. It is proper for the stage pirates in *Peter Pan* to refer to
a future meeting "below," but they would shock the audience if
they used the more realistic and theologically canonical word.
It is a similar desire to avoid the direct admission of a disagree-
able truth, *viz.,* that judges are not merely umpires but also
make the law, that has led to the great host of legal fictions in
the Anglo-American common law. It would be absurd to regard
these fictions as false propositions. They are rather resolutions to
extend certain legal rights. When the courts insist that the high
seas are in the parish of Mary Le Bone in London, they mean
to assert not an absurd impossibility, but merely that they will
take jurisdiction of acts occurring on the high seas as if they

had occurred in London; and in doing so they may be perfectly consistent. An adopted son is not a natural son, but he is entitled to the same rights. So with the fiction of the legal (not natural) personality of corporations. Though these fictions border on, they can be distinguished from, myths which are genuinely believed, and from pious frauds which are intended to deceive in the aid of a good cause. The Roman jurists explained such fictions by means of the Greek philosophic distinction between convention and nature.

Why, however, does not the law use accurate expressions instead of asserting as a fact that which need not be so? Why assert that a corporation *is* a person, instead of saying that a certain group of rights and duties are analogous, to some extent, to those of a natural person? Why say that the United States Embassy in China or on a boat at sea is on American soil, when we mean that certain legal relations in or concerning it are to be treated according to the law of the United States? The answer, in part, is that the practical convenience of brevity outweighs the theoretic gain of greater accuracy. But more important is the fact that at all times, and not merely in "primitive" society where legislatures are not functioning, the law must grow by assimilating the new to old situations, and in moments of innovation we cling, all the more, to old linguistic forms.

From the point of view of social policy fictions are, like eloquence, important in giving the emotional drive to propositions that we wish to see accepted. They can be used to soften the shock of innovation (as when the courts protect a man's vines by calling them *trees*), or to keep up a pleasant veneration for truths which we have abandoned (as when we give new allegoric meaning to old theologic dogmas that are no longer tenable). The confusions, however, between the literal and conventional meaning have been a fruitful source of fallacious reasoning. For if fictions sometimes facilitate change they often hinder it by cultivating an undue regard for the past. If social interest in truth were to prevail, we should in our educational and social policies encourage greater regard for literal accuracy even when it hurts national pride and social sensibilities. But no one has seriously suggested penalizing rhetoric and poetic eloquence in the discussion of social issues. The interest in truth is in fact not as great as in the preservation of cherished beliefs, even though the latter involve ultimate illusions whose pleasantness is more or less temporary.

3. *Abstractions*

In the recent reaction against physical science and its assumptions of an independent reality to which our ideas must conform, if they are to be true, idealistic philosophers and theologians, aided by some humanistic pragmatists and dogmatic positivists, have pressed the point that many of the concepts of natural science such as law, cause, atom, ether, and the like, are mere fictions having no correspondence in nature, though they aid us in controlling things for practical purposes. In the social sciences, as well, there has developed a similar tendency to regard abstractions like social law, the economic motive, legal sovereignty, social order, and the like as fictions that have no objective significance in real life.

Hegelians, positivists, and the followers of James and Bergson are united today in characterizing the abstract as unreal, and Vaihinger classifies all abstractions as fictions or semi-fictions. In the face of so much unanimity in diverse quarters it seems hazardous to put forth a simple denial. Let us, therefore, admit, as we all can, that abstractions are not real if the real is defined as that which is concrete and not abstract; but let us also insist on the fact—for fact it seems to me in spite of the ideaphobia of Schopenhauer, James, and Bergson—that we do gain real knowledge by valid reasoning about abstractions, that mathematical computation, for instance, does actually help to extend our knowledge of the factual world. We can insist on this while granting that there is a certain *salte mortale* between reasoning about abstractions and its application to any actual concrete situation.

This *salte mortale* is perhaps the reason which makes modern enthusiasts characterize as fictional such a concept as "the economic man" of Ricardo. Let us admit that no man has as yet ever acted from purely economic motives. This, however, in no way denies the force of Ricardo's reasoning or makes his deductions inapplicable to actual economic phenomena. The assertion that men are not actuated solely by economic motives does not deny that economic motives do exist and that while we cannot completely isolate them in fact, we can compute their consequences, just as we can compute that certain physical consequences will happen to a man solely because of his weight, or to certain substances because of their electric or thermal properties.

The distrust of abstract reasoning thus rests upon two grounds: (1) the chasm between what might be called the realms of mathematics and history, or of logical validity and brute existence, and (2) upon the dogma that every proposition asserts the inherence of a quality in a substance, or of an attribute in an existing subject.

(1) All reasoning about abstractions takes the form of a universal proposition which can be put either into the hypothetical form or as a categoric assertion of the necessary or invariant connection between two elements. Now, as Hume and Kant have insisted, no number of historic instances can establish a universal or invariant relation. The existence of such invariant relations in the various sciences is an hypothesis, not proved *a priori* as Kant thought, but verified by the course of experience. Whenever we apply a theorem concerning an abstract entity, say a geometric sphere, to an actual body such as the earth or the sun, we make the *salte mortale* of equating an abstract and a concrete entity (in the proposition: this is a sphere). Such a proposition can never be absolutely free from error; but the actual discovery of divergences never can throw doubt upon our abstract theorems, because we can explain the discrepancy by additional hypotheses, and the history of human science has shown this method to be the most reliable of all human instru-

ments. From this point of view, abstractions may be viewed as methodologic resolutions, or determinations to look at objects in certain ways. To be scientific we must carry out our resolutions consistently; and the laws of consistency are not arbitrarily made by our fiat, but are imposed upon us by the world in which we live, or the world which we study.

(2) The second reason why abstractions, which are parts or phases of the real world, are regarded as unreal is due to the Aristotelian assumption that every proposition asserts the inherence of the predicate in the subject and that the ultimately real subject is an individual. From these two propositions we can get either a brute pluralism—a Leibnizian world of many individuals, but as no one thing can be a predicate of another there can be no real connection between them—or an ineffable monism of the Bradleyan type in which the ultimate or the absolute subject forever eludes us. From this dilemma we escape through the modern relational view of the nature of a proposition—which metaphysically means that not things but a complex of things-in-relation is the subject-matter of science. From this point of view propositions about abstractions and abstract relations no more falsify reality than do propositions about particulars. All propositions are more or less elliptical—as we can see by an analysis of the nature of language and signs. If I say, "Jones is a wise or good man," this is clearly not true without qualification. We mean wise in some things, for the most part, as human beings go, etc. The more logically conscientious we become, the more need for adding qualifications. But these qualifications need not always be expressed, because they are not sufficiently important or relevant for the purpose of communication. Precisely similar considerations hold in regard to abstract assertions. The statement that heat expands objects is true only if we add "under the same pressure" and "provided we do not apply this to water between 32 degrees and 38 degrees Fahrenheit," etc. The degree of completeness necessary depends upon the purpose and circumstances of the proposition as a communication.

4. *Construction and Hypotheses*

We have treated metaphors, ceremonial expressions, and abstractions under the heading of fictions partly because they are
generally so called, and partly because they all illustrate the
fallacies into which we fall if we press the rules of the traditional
logic without taking certain precautions. These precautions may
all be deduced from the rule that the truth of a proposition
holds only in its proper universe of discourse (or type in Russell's
logic). This rule holds, indeed, of all propositions. Metaphors,
ceremonial expressions, and abstractions do not differ from ordinary propositions in principle, since ordinary propositions are
all more or less metaphorical, conventional, and abstract. However, there is current a sharp distinction between fact and fiction—the former as something which we find, the latter as something that we create. In the last few decades, especially since the
publication of Vaihinger's *Philosophie des Als Ob,* there has
been an increased general recognition of the importance of fiction as construction in science. But the subject has been be-
clouded by the monistic mania. By trying to show that everything is a mental construction, the distinction between fact and
fiction is really obliterated.

It must be admitted that while the distinction between making and finding something is very sharp in the physical realm, it
is by no means so clear in other fields. Did the Romans find or
invent their legal system? Did the Greeks find or invent geometric science? We always speak of finding the solution to all sorts
of problems and even great mechanical inventors testify that
they find their inventions, that the sought-for device sometimes
"flashes upon them," and most often they "stumble upon it"
while looking for something else. It may be objected that the
expressions just used are more or less metaphoric; but the fact is
that whenever we apply to mental objects the categories that we
usually and confidently apply to physical objects, we necessarily
resort to metaphors. A complete clarification of this point de-

mands a re-examination of what is meant by applying the categories of identity, determination, and creation to mental objects. Reserving this re-examination for a future occasión, I shall here barely refer to some of the more superficial aspects of scientific construction that seem to have no counterpart in the real world and are generally regarded as fictional.

Vaihinger divides all fictions into genuine fictions which involve self-contradiction, and semi-fictions which are constructions not in agreement with reality or fact. His work is characterized by wide but superficial and grossly inaccurate learning and is dominated by what we·called earlier the monistic mania. With amazing industry he has gathered a most imposing list of what he calls genuine fictions. Nevertheless, there ought to be no hesitation in flatly denying that any of them do involve self-contradiction. If they did, no fruitful consequences could be drawn from them and they would not have the explanatory power which makes them so useful in science. But what is worse is that in trying to stretch the notion of fiction to cover everything, he leaves no room for a valid distinction between truth and falsehood, between fiction and reality. If identity and difference, unity and plurality, and other fundamental categories are fictional, then every one of Vaihinger's assertions about *reality*, the *order of sensations, convenience* and *fictions* is itself fictional, and we are landed in a self-destructive nihilism. All this, however, grows out of his unnecessary and mythical dualism between purely active thought and absolutely passive sensations, as if they belonged to two different worlds. For we should realize that the abstract objects of thought, such as numbers, *law, perfectly straight lines,* etc., are real parts of nature (even though they do not exist as *particular* things but as the *relations* or *transformations* of such particulars), so that none of the so-called fictions of science in any way falsify its results. Because numbers or ratios are abstractions it does not follow that there is anything fictional in the assertion that the earth has *one* moon, or that the *rate* of infant mortality has recently decreased. The supposition that there is, arises from a false notion of scientific procedure and its results. It arises from forgetting that abstractions are real parts, phases, or elements in things or their relations, though they are not identical in all respects with the things. The contentions of the fictionalists, however, supply us with cautions against false interpretations of scientific procedures and results. Abstractions are real parts, phases or elements of things, or their relations. To identify them with *things* is a widespread fallacy which may be called reification.

The typical fiction which Vaihinger and others most often cite is the so-called imaginary number, $\sqrt{-1}$. As in ordinary algebra there are no numbers whose square can be negative, this is triumphantly adduced as a clear example of a useful device based on a logically impossible entity. Modern mathematics, however, has made it clear that $\sqrt{-1}$ is no more imaginary or self-contradictory than $\sqrt{2}$, which is still called irrational, surd, or absurd. Starting with certain useful conventions as to pairs of numbers, $\sqrt{-1}$ becomes a most useful clue to the properties of certain fields of force, so that it is hard to imagine how Maxwell's modern electric theory could possibly have been developed without the previous work of Gauss and Hamilton on the functions of $\sqrt{-1}$. Logically, similar considerations hold with regard to the argument that self-contradiction inheres in the notion of infinite number or of infinitesimal magnitude. Modern mathematics has removed the basis for such arguments. One hears nowadays that the ether is a fiction which involves contradictory qualities. This, also, is simply not true. The ether is an hypothetical entity, the existence of which follows from certain assumptions such as the law of the conservation of energy. Some of its properties are undoubtedly very unusual, and modern electro-magnetic theory makes most of the mechanical models or analogies of it useless. But it is not at all self-contradictory—certainly not when it is in any way a useful explanation.

The reason which leads so many to regard entities like $\sqrt{-1}$ as fictional is that they can see no substantial counterpart to them in the objective world. But if we forego the prepossession with existential entities and adopt the relational logic, there is no difficulty in pointing to the exact place in the objective world where the $\sqrt{-1}$ is to be found. We only have to keep in mind that it is not a thing nor the property of a thing, but a relation or transformation of things. The difficulty of explaining how that which is a pure fiction can explain or serve as a clue to the processes of nature is a difficulty which only the exclusive substance-attribute logic has to face. There seems to me no difficulty in maintaining, if you wish, the copy-theory of truth provided you admit that the world contains, besides things and their qualities, also relations and processes between them, and that the fruitfulness of science consists precisely in not copying the qualities of things but in grouping and symbolizing those relations or processes which most frequently repeat themselves.

That this view can actually be carried out—that we can show all the fictions or constructions of science to rest on a real basis to the extent that they are in any way useful as explanations— can be fully proved only by actually writing a new and complete logic of science. A most cursory survey of the field, however, is sufficient for the present purpose.

To the extent that scientific fictions or constructions serve to explain anything, they logically serve as hypotheses. These hypotheses may relate to entities which are empirically discoverable, or to entities which are not directly discoverable. Ignoring the former hypotheses which are not generally regarded as fictional, we may subdivide the latter into hypotheses which seem to be contrary to fact, and hypotheses which seem to be so neutral to the realm of fact that the existence of their subject-matter can never be directly shown or disproved.

Of hypotheses which seem contrary to fact, the existence of perfectly free bodies, or of frictionless steam engines, are the best examples. Newton's free bodies, which are the subject of the first law of motion, cannot have any existence because of the law of gravity which comes into operation as soon as there are two particles, and the existence of a frictionless steam engine would be contrary to all thermo-dynamic experience. Yet reason-

ing about free bodies and frictionless engines is the very foundation of mechanics and thermo-dynamics, and the reason for this
is that the relations and processes denoted by freely moving
bodies, or by frictionless engines, are of the widest occurrence—
only they do not occur in isolation, but always in conjunction
with other elements.

The results of these processes of abstraction and classification
have been called neglective fictions because, it is claimed, the
class *man* does not exist and only individuals do. But it cannot
be denied that such statements as John is a man can have significance only if the predicate denotes something really common to
a number of individuals. Even such an artificial classification of
governments as that of Aristotle cannot be called fictional merely
because actual governments do not conform to it. For existing
governments may be mixed forms or combinations of the elements of monarchy, aristocracy and democracy and their per-
versions, and our classification helps us to recognize such mixed
forms because of the elements they contain. The fact that certain elements always occur in conjunction with others and never
in isolation is no more argument against their reality than the
fact that no one can be a brother or a creditor without being
other things is an argument against the possibility of having
these abstract characteristics. Science must abstract some elements
and neglect others because not all things that exist together are
relevant to each other.

Another way of looking at neglective fictions such as perfectly rigid bodies, perfect distribution and the like, is to view
them as ideal limits. No one thing in nature corresponds to
these, but things do differ in degrees of rigidity or homogeneity
and may be arranged into a series according to the degree of
rigidity or homogeneity they possess. Perfect regidity would then
be the character which all the members of the series possessed
to some degree, and on the basis of which they are ordered in the
series. It is the principle of order of such a series.

From this point of view we need not admit that there is
anything specially subjective about the ideal elements or cases

which abound in science—perfect circles, absolute rigidity of matter, absolute or ideal justice, and other entities of that sort. There is nothing to prevent ideal entities of this sort representing actual relations between things or, more frequently, complexes of things expressed in judgments. While there exist no free bodies, all existing bodies do move in such a way that we can find the part played by inertia or what would happen if all other forces ceased to act; similarly, while no actual engine is frictionless, we can from certain data compute the part that friction plays in the total work of any engine.

This enables us to dispose of those positivists, like Levy-Bruhl, A. Levi, Rolin, Tourtoulon, or G. G. Cox in this country, who deny the possibility of any normative science such as ethics. Science, they say, deals only with facts; ethics is an affair of individual opinion as to what is desirable. As, however, there is an obvious difference between enlightened and unenlightened judgment as to what is desirable, these positivists can retain their position only by distinguishing between the art and science of morals. Science, they tell us, shows us the laws according to which happenings are concatenated. To pick one's way amid these laws is an art or practical wisdom. This, however, evades the real issue, which is whether the question of the consistency of certain ethical judgments is or is not a legitimate question of science. To call it an art is not to answer this question in the negative, since all science is, in a sense, an intellectual art—the art of building up a system of consistent judgments.

Neutral hypotheses, those of which the subject-matter can never be directly proved or disproved, are very numerous in all sciences. Thus the old-fashioned books on economics would begin by imagining one or more people landed on a desert island, just as the older theories of law and politics begin with an imaginary social contract, or modern mathematical physicists ask you to imagine a creature in a one- or two-dimensional space. Reasoning from such imaginary constructions is, indeed, often confusing because we do not form a very clear idea of what it is that we are asked to imagine. But there is nothing fallacious in the method of such arguments. Much abuse has been heaped on the "social contract" as a fiction. If it is taken as an historical fact it is a myth. This, however, is not the way it was conceived by the great thinkers of the seventeenth and eighteenth centuries. To them it was a logical device for analyzing actual complex social processes. If we apply the term "state of nature" to human conduct apart from the influence of laws, we can regard our actual social relations as those of a state of nature modified by contracts. The analogy is helpful only to the limited extent to which it is true. The social contract is really not an hypothesis as to what actually happened, but a concept of social transformation. Concepts of this sort are like the auxiliary lines in a drawing or the parallels of latitude and longitude which we use in drawing maps. If one were to tell us that to draw a map of North America we should begin with drawing a certain triangle, then draw certain other lines, etc., it would be absurd to object that North America is not and never was a triangle. The triangle can, in truth, represent the relations between a point in Greenland, one in Alaska, and one at the Isthmus of Panama; and by beginning with these points the relation of others to them could be indicated in the manner directed. The map will never be a complete picture of North America, but it can be perfectly true on the scale indicated. Fictions, like maps and charts, are useful precisely because they do not copy the whole, but only the significant relations. These relations are identical in analogous cases; and we perceive and master the flux of phenomena only when we see running through it the threads of identity.

VI

On Probability

1. *Theories of Probability*

Judged by its indispensable role in our daily practical judgments, as well as in the procedure of natural science, the concept of probability is one of the most important in the whole field of philosophy. Since the failure of the romantic *Naturphilosophie* to derive infallible knowledge of nature *a priori,* and since the discovery that other than Euclidean geometry may be true in the physical world, it has become generally evident that all our factual knowledge (that is, all except purely formal or mathematical considerations), is only probable in the sense that we cannot *prove* the contrary to be absolutely impossible.

To an increasing extent, we now find the idea of probability developed by logicians, mathematicians, physicists, biologists, and statisticians; but, with the honorable exceptions of Leibniz, Cournot, and Peirce, philosophers have given it scant attention. Possibly the chief reason for this is the uneliminable religious and moral craving for absolute certainty, so that anything that fails to support it is relegated to the "merely empirical" realm. It is curious to note that the sharp separation between philosophy and empirical inquiry, leading to a neglect of philosophic interest in probability, is also maintained by such a thoroughgoing anti-supernaturalist as Bertrand Russell.

Theories of probability, like so many other theories, may be traced back to Aristotle, who seems to have first used the word εἰκοσία as a technical term to denote the subject of our investigation, and who treats the problem of probability under the head of Dialectics. As a follower of Plato, Aristotle restricts *knowledge* to that which is necessarily true. But unlike Plato, and perhaps influenced by Democritus, he gives a more positive role to *opinion*. Some opinions are better than others because they are held more frequently or by those who are well informed or trained in their particular subject. If probability is not in the field of necessity (ἀνάγκη) it is at least in the field of law (νόμος). Arguments from probabilities are thus persuasive though not conclusive. The probable is thus the problematic, which etymologically connotes a question thrown at one. At any rate, it is certain that the word *probability* comes directly from the Latin *probare*—to probe or prove. In that respect Locke's view of probability seems to be substantially like that of Aristotle. For Locke, also, views probability as a character of inference which lacks a basis in that which is always and demonstrably true— for instance, the knowledge that the ordinary man not trained in geometry has of the fact that the sum of the angles of a triangle is equal to two right angles, when such knowledge is based on the authority of those who know.

Modern theories of probability may be generally characterized as either subjective or objective, i.e., dealing either with the character of our beliefs or opinions, or with the character of the objective evidence for these beliefs or opinions. Though writers on probability often more or less consciously combine these points of view, the distinction between them is in the main clear enough. Venn's "Logic of Chance" may be taken as representative of the objective point of view, while DeMorgan's treatise on Probability may be taken as typical of the other point of view, which is often referred to as the conceptualist point of view. The whole modern psychologic tendency puts the emphasis on the mental phase of the beliefs called probable, and this is reinforced by popular discourse, which has many expressions for degrees of probability, such as, "Highly probable," "very likely," "almost certain," "improbable," "not at all likely," and others. We say, "I am almost certain"; "I am quite sure"; "I am convinced"; "It seems to me"; etc. But the whole tendency of modern logic and exact science demands a definiteness in probable judgments which does not seem to be offered by any differences in the intensity of belief. Keynes in his great treatise on Probability endeavored to set up as a standard beliefs that he calls rational, but apart from material evidence the concept of rationality does not seem very clear.

Objective theories frequently begin with the concept of possibility, and consider the number of various equally possible but mutually exclusive happenings, but the concept of "equally possible," unless further qualified, is essentially obscure.

Events are possible or impossible. There seem to be no intermediate states between the two.

Thus probability is a category of inference that may be sharply distinguished from the kind called necessary, certain or (to avoid psychologic entanglements) conclusively demonstrative. An inference is rigorously demonstrable if it can be shown that it is impossible for the premises to be true and the conclusion to be false. Thus we prove a theorem in geometry when we show that it is impossible for it to be false if certain previously specified propositions (axioms and their derivatives) are true. Not all inferences, however, are of that kind. Indeed most inferences that we make do not take that form. Thus, that no man has hitherto attained the age of two hundred years does not prove it impossible for one of us to live that long. Yet that is certainly evidence of a sort that cannot be ignored in science or in practice. The proposition, "All Presidents of the United States have been Protestants," does not prove that "The next President will also be one." But we should not regard these two propositions as altogether irrelevant to each other. The first is evidence of some sort for the second, though it falls short of being conclusive. We call such inferences from partial evidence probable.

Against the foregoing view, which restricts probability to classes or kinds of inference, it may be objected that in actual usage we do mean something by the probability of a single proposition or event, that we are in fact primarily interested not in the probability of the inference but in the probable truth of propositions for which we do not know or even seek any evidence.

Actual popular usage, however, is not decisive for purposes of philosophy, else philosophic issues would all be settled by consulting a reliable dictionary. In this case there is an obvious logical contradiction between holding a proposition to be by definition either true or false and then speaking as if probability could be characteristic of it. Probability when measured is a fraction and a proposition cannot be fractionally true.

He who characterizes a popular expression as illogical or inaccurate does well to indicate the natural source of the inaccuracy. If we contend that it is strictly meaningless to speak of the probability of a proposition, how is it that men do use that expression and are certain that they do mean something by it? The answer to this can be readily apprehended if we remember that in ordinary discourse we generally take certain things for granted and the full meaning of what we say is to be found not in the actual words used nor even in what is consciously present to the mind but rather in what reflection finds to be implied. Thus, we speak of a body as at rest or in motion without stopping to indicate with respect to what it is at rest or in motion. If I say, "The car is in motion," we generally understand, and need not add, "with reference to the earth." We thus get into the habit of viewing the expression, "The car is in motion," as a complete statement, whereas reflection shows that by itself it is incomplete. Similarly, we speak of "the probability of a proposition" without specifying with reference to what evidence it is probable. We may, therefore, continue to speak of the probability of a proposition, as an abbreviated expression for its probability relative to our total knowledge or body of propositions which serve as evidence for it.

According to the orthodox theory of Russell and Whitehead's *Principia*, when the premises are true and our reasoning valid, we can assert our conclusions categorically and thus drop the "if" or the premises. Certain difficulties are inherent in this view, specifically, when applied to regions where the meaning of a proposition obviously depends on the context or system in which it occurs and of which the premises are an integral part. But however that may be, we certainly cannot ignore or drop the premises of a probable inference. For the same proposition may have different probability-values according to the different sets of propositions which are offered as evidence for it. Thus, the probability that a defendant in a court of law is guilty may vary in the course of the presentation of the evidence for or against him.

Keynes, in his treatise on probability, takes this relation between premise or evidence and conclusion as indefinable. Others, like Bradley, treat it as a matter of intuition. Now we need not deny the varying force of different arguments to a mind trained in the weighing of evidence. But since all admit that probability is a matter of degree, and in some (but not all) cases measurable, it is of the utmost scientific importance to define it so as to give meaning to some criterion or verifiable way of distinguishing the more probable from the less probable. It is the great advantage of the frequency theory of probability that it enables us to do this in many cases. According to this view one class of premises defined by a single propositional function is more probable than another if it will give us a larger proportion of true conclusions. And any proposition is more probable than not if the evidence in its favor is greater than that against it.

The notion of a proportion of the conclusions being true needs some clarification to remove seeming conflicts with the orthodox (and correct) view; (1) that the consequences of a true proposition must always be true, and (2) that no proposition, whether it is a conclusion or not, can be sometimes true and sometimes false. Reflection shows that as to the first point there is no conflict, because the orthodox rule applies only to rigorous demonstrative inference; and as to the second point, the conflict disappears when we remember that all inference, whether probable or demonstrative, is formal, i.e., applies to classes of propositions. It is well known that the probative force of a syllogism does not depend on the specific terms that occur in it but will hold of any triplet used in a similar manner. A syllogism thus gives us a class of conclusions which are all true if the respective premises are true. A probable inference gives us a class of conclusions of which only a part are true. Thus if there is a rule that no student of my college can be under fifteen years of age, I can conclude that to be true of *every* individual student. But if eight-tenths of all the students of my college are over fifteen years of age, I can say that there is a probability of eight-tenths that any student who leaves the building is of that age, i.e., eight-tenths of such specific conclusions will be true. This ratio will hold if for the term *student* we substitute *instructor, janitor, visitor,* or anyone else. Note that there is no *necessary* inference from a proposition or premise concerning distribution in a class, to a conclusion concerning a single individual member of it. But what we do assert is the relative frequency or number of times such specific conclusions will be true if the given premise is true.

Of course our evidence may not always be as definite as in the foregoing examples. We may argue that it is more probable than not that Jones will recover from his injury, because nowadays most of those so injured recover. But we may also argue that there is some probability that he will recover even though we do not know what proportion of the injured these recoveries constitute. This, however, only means that we often rely on evidence insufficient to give us a determinate probability but enough to establish an indeterminate one.

It will be noticed that in order to use a number of observed instances as evidence for the probability of another case, we must assume the latter as well as the former to be members of a common class—else there would be no logical connection at all. If your child's recovery is evidence of any sort, even of the smallest weight, for the recovery of my child, it must be because the two are alike in some factor that is relevant to the recovery.

This brings us to the question of the probability of an inference as to a universal proposition or "law" on the basis of a number of observed instances of it. Keynes and others have raised serious objections against the possibility of applying the frequency theory to such inductive inference. But these objections seem to me to apply only if we have an inadequate conception as to the logical force of induction.

We must go even further than Keynes and reject the common notion—on which rests LaPlace's classic formula and most theorems as to inverse probability—that the probability of an induction always increases with the number of observed instances.

Consider the usual illustration of induction given in our logic texts, viz., that of the sun rising. Is it true that the more often we have seen it rise the more probable it is that we will see it rise again? If that were the case there would be a greater probability of the man who has seen it rise 36,000 times living another day, than the man who had seen it rise 3,600 times—which is absurd. Mill, himself the strongest defender of the claims of induction, admitted with characteristic candor that in some cases a few instances are far more probative than a much larger number of instances in other situations.

Yet surely we cannot altogether dismiss the view that the wider the experimental basis of any universal proposition, the greater its probability. What can be better evidence for a universal proposition than actual instances in which experience shows it to be true?

These conflicting considerations show that the traditional account of the evidential force of induction is too simple and that we need to introduce some qualification or distinction.

We must, to begin with, make the obvious distinction between the initial probability of any universal proposition (which we can consider as an hypothesis) and the probability added to it when we find that its specific consequences are true. The necessity for the latter kind of evidence should not blind us to the presence of the former. Any generalization or hypothesis which, in the course of a scientific investigation, suggests itself as possibly covering all the facts is likely to have some analogies in its favor or to be an instance of some more general proposition. It, therefore, derives some probability from the latter. Thus the initial probability of any generalization about a newly discovered species of plants or animals would depend on the more general propositions of biology. And we always do start with previous knowledge if we wish to make progress. Thus it would not occur to a reasonable priest whose first three penitents were murderers to generalize and attribute that trait to all laymen. The overwhelming probability (or practical certainty) that all men are mortal rests not on the actual number of human deaths any of us have observed but more on certain wider general propositions about the nature of animal life. It is true, of course, that the latter propositions have a wider range of confirmatory instances; but the distinction between the initial probability of any universal proposition and that which it acquires by confirmation is still a valid one.

It should be noticed that in the very process of gathering confirmatory instances we must depend upon prior universals in order to be able to identify the instances. Consider a familiar example. An urn contains a large number of balls. They are mixed up and I draw out a number of them which are found to be blue in all cases. I infer a probability that all are of that color. All the evidence conforms to our hypothesis and there is no evidence against it. Yet we should not regard this as at all reliable if we did not know something about the constitution of collections of balls in urns, and the infrequency with which an urn containing balls of differing colors, thoroughly mixed up, will contain those of a special color in just such a position as to be drawn first. Without such prior knowledge we should be arguing from certain observations to others that we know nothing of, and there is no logical magic by which we can extract knowledge or evidence of probability or anything else from pure ignorance.

The foregoing considerations will enable us to deal with the question raised but not answered by Mill, viz., why in some cases a few instances have greater weight than a much larger number in other situations.

Thus one or two tests of the alkalinity of a new chemical compound may establish it with a very high degree of probability, while innumerable uncontradicted instances of white swans or pious botanists will not afford such high probability of all swans being white or all botanists pious. The explanation of this is to be found in our prior knowledge or assumption that the color of animals or the piety of men is rather variable. The probative force or evidential value of an induction therefore depends not simply on the number of specific instances observed, but on the degree of homogeneity of our class, i.e., on the extent to which instances or samples are typical or representative of the whole class. This point is of the utmost importance in guarding against the fallacy of selection.

Suppose I examine a large number of Negroes and find that they have certain characteristics, say certain peculiarities of diction. The inference that all Negroes will have that trait is subject to the fallacy of selection. All the Negroes examined may have been of a certain social class, or of a certain geographic location, or my particular mode of questioning them may have helped to bring about the particular response. My generalization is then true not of Negroes, as such, but rather of any people belonging to a particular class or location, or responding in certain ways under certain conditions—so that other Negroes will be altogether different. If I think of such possible alternative explanations of the results I will use the methods of agreement, difference, and concomitant variations to test my generalization. But if I do not know what factors are relevant and responsible for the result, and rely on a large number taken at random, I rely only on the hope that special circumstances will not operate in all my cases. A large number may therefore not be as probative as a smaller number subjected to critical tests. That is why statistical or purely empirical formulae or laws do not have as much weight in science as those that are rationally derived.

We may thus conclude that the probability of inductive inference depends on two factors: (1) Every generalization which does not comprehend the entire universe is an instance of a more general proposition that may have a certain probability or be known to be true in a number of instances. To this extent the probability of an induction clearly conforms to the frequency theory as applied to the quasi-deductive examples used above. (2) Though confirmatory instances are always needed to meet possible doubt of our general proposition or of those on which it rests, no number of actual instances is sufficient (in the cases of unlimited classes) to give us determinate probability. For we cannot by mere enumeration tell what proportion of the totality is constituted by our finite collection. Instances alone can in such cases give us at best only an indeterminate probability, and there is only a bare minimum of scientific value in showing that a certain proposition is barely probable, i.e., not impossible. What is of greater actual value in scientific procedure is to show that any generalization or hypothesis has a greater probability than any of its possible rival alternatives; and this is achieved by showing that it holds in a greater number of properly *comparable* cases.

We have hinted before that the great advantage of the frequency theory of probability is that it enables us to give a definite account of how to verify probability theorems. The latter is a great *desideratum* in view of the loose way in which the term verification has been generally used.

According to the traditional account, we verify an hypothesis when its consequences are found to be confirmed by sensory experience. (Seeing is believing, but touching is the naked truth.) This mode of reasoning, however, is the well-known fallacy of arguing from the affirmation of the consequence. And it seems rather scandalous for logic as a science of consistency to maintain such a double standard, condemning an inference as a fallacy in the part called deductive and glorifying it as verification in the part called inductive. We may of course remove the scandal by insisting on the distinction between proof and verification. When offered as a conclusive proof for the truth of the antecedent,

the argument from the affirmation of the consequence is a fallacy; but when offered as a verification or as evidence of its probability, it is relevant and generally the only means of testing its
truth. But even so, a realistic account of verification must take
a relativistic form and envisage not a single hypothesis which
can be verified by confirmation—a task too easy to be of much
scientific value—but rather a process of weighing rival hypotheses. If we have two or more competing hypotheses and we can
make a crucial experiment or observation which confirms one
and disproves the other, then the one that is confirmed has thus
been demonstrated to be a better account of the facts so far
known. Verification, in other words, does not strictly prove a
hypothesis to be true—the history of science shows well verified
hypotheses to have finally turned out to be false—but it gives
us logical reason for regarding one as more probable than the
other, since it explains more of the facts.

The prevailing account of verification contemplates universal
propositions that predict certain uniform results and exclude
others as impossible. They can therefore be refuted by a single
instance to the contrary. But this does not apply to propositions
that assert a probability. If, following Maxwell and Boltzman,
we assert that the probability of a cubic centimeter of gas dividing itself into two distinct parts of unequal temperatures, is less
than one in a quadrillion, the actual occurrence of such an event
will not constitute a refutation of our assertion. For the improbable is not ruled out as impossible. We are thus tempted to
draw a sharp distinction between the verification of laws such
as those of classical mechanics and the verification of statistical
probabilities, on the ground that no crucial experiment or observation can refute the statement of a probability. If, however,
we consistently adhere to the frequency theory, we realize that
the test of a probability statement requires not a single observation but a large number, since probability judgments are directly concerned with groups of phenomena. If the particles of a
gas did frequently divide themselves into two parts of different
temperatures, we should have a right to question any theory

which assigns this occurrence such a low probability. If a penny falls head forty-nine or fifty times in fifty throws, we may well question whether the proper probability of its falling head in any one instance is one-half. According to our analysis, to assert the latter is to predict that it will fall head as often as tail. This is a material assertion which must ultimately rest on experience, and it would be absurd to contend that what has been affirmed on the basis of past experience cannot be denied on the basis of further experience. On the theory of fair dealing, it is extremely improbable that my opponent will hold four aces twice in succession. When that actually happens, the hypothesis of fair dealing is not refuted; but we may well reconsider it, and entertain the contrary one as a more satisfactory account of the situation. We certainly would do so if that hand were repeated more often.

It may well be objected that this way of verifying a probability is very unprecise, that it offers no definite canon of telling when a run is sufficiently long to serve as a test. Abstractly stated, this objection is certainly sound. But we must not forget that the actual choice between mechanical hypotheses which make universal assertions—for example the choice between the Ptolemaic and the Copernican astronomy, between the corpuscular and the wave theory of light, between the continental and Faraday's theory of electricity—were not as easily decided by crucial experiments as the popular histories assert. Despite Lavoisier's experiments, the phlogiston theory continued to be held for a considerable time, and Galileo's supposed refutation of Aristotle's theory of gravitation by dropping two objects from the tower of Pisa is rather mythical, for under the actual conditions of height, atmospheric friction, etc., such an experiment could not have been decisive. Science, in fact, depends on cables of many strands rather than on chains of many links. It is wise, therefore, to insist on the real and important distinction between the verification of universal propositions and the verification of assertions of probability, but also to guard against making the distinction too sharp.

The foregoing reflections will help us to consider the nature of the *a priori* in judgments of probability.

Reasoning on matters of probability involves a remarkable amount of reliance on *a priori* considerations. (By *a priori*, I mean general principles which are not based on the observation of the course of events in the special field to which they are applied, and are incapable of being refuted by any empirical fact in that field.) Thus, the certainty with which people assert that the probability of a penny falling head is one-half generally rests on no accurate formulation of previous experience, and indeed often involves a resolution to ignore experience, as in the case of the astronomer Proctor, who insists that if a penny has fallen head fifty times running, the probability of the next throw being head is still one-half. This is a position which, as has been indicated, cannot be refuted because we can, if we wish, explain all departures from it in terms of specific disturbing causes. Propositions of this sort are suggested by the general principles of symmetry and initial simplicity, but they can justify themselves logically by the fact that they enable us to organize the phenomena in their field into some coherent order or system. They are, in that sense, methodological postulates. The chance of a penny falling head, because it is an illustration of the principle of insufficient reason or indifference, serves to exemplify the use of the methodologic postulate. According to the principle of indifference, it is supposed that we have a right to assert or assign to each side of the penny a probability of one-half, in so far as we know nothing which will enable us to decide between two alternatives. We need not go into the absurd consequences to which this often leads. They have been pointed out by Von Kries, Keynes, Fischer, and others. This example is referred to, in passing, as an illustration of our readiness to build calculations on the basis of complete ignorance. This is also true of the readiness with which mathematicians and statisticians, lay or expert, are ready to assume that events whose causes or determinants are unknown are not only equi-probable but also independent of each other. All reasoning as to probability which expresses itself in numbers involves *inter alia* an assumption of equi-probability. For, to assert that a certain arrangement *A* has a numerical probability or is more probable than an arrangement *B*, it is not enough to assert that *A* has a number of complexions or possibilities. We must also assume that all of these complexions are equi-probable. But the judgment of equi-probability is a prediction as to the course of material events, to wit: that they will occur with the same relative frequency. Such a prediction may be based on the evidence of past experience or we may prefer the hypothesis of equi-probability because it seems the simplest. As we saw before, neither of these types of evidence is conclusive, but psychologically we seem predisposed to regard the simplicity of our hypothesis as offering a greater or indeed an absolute certainty.

This tendency to treat matters of fact on purely *a priori* considerations without any recourse to verification seems to be the prevailing attitude in most mathematical treatments of probability. The mathematician is perfectly justified in saying that if I assume that any card is as likely to turn up as any other, and if one deal is completely independent of the previous one, then certain combinations or hands have certain determinate probabilities or relative frequencies. But it is surely not within the realm of pure mathematics to determine that these assumptions are true in the actual shuffling of cards. In brief, no numerical determination of probability is logically possible without a material or factual assumption as to equi-probability, and the latter is often quite arbitrary. Consider, for instance, the famous problem of LaPlace in regard to the probability of a chance arrangement resulting in all the planets having their angles of inclination to the ecliptic, such as actually prevail in our solar system. The problem cannot be intelligently dealt with without an assumption as to what arrangements are equi-probable, and it is by no means clear what our starting point here should be.

We cannot build up any natural science without hypotheses or anticipations of nature which go beyond past experience; and hypotheses which we have called *a priori*, because they cannot be refuted by finite experience, are indispensable in the determination of probabilities as in dealing with most empirical and contingent material. But if we enlarge, as we must, our concept of verification, even these *a priori* hypotheses are verifiable; for we can formulate alternatives to them whenever they deal with factual situations. And over large stretches or series of experiments, we may decide that one of the hypotheses serves the purpose of our science better than another.

The same emphasis on relativity must be maintained when we speak of the probability not of propositions but of natural events. No event, we must insist, is in itself probable. The defendant did or did not commit the murder. It will rain tomorrow or it will not. Probability does not belong to an event in itself, but only to the event in its representative capacity so far as it is a member of a class of events which stands in a certain relation of relative frequency to another class. This may not be what the common man actually has in mind. But we are concerned not with descriptive psychology but with logical requirements for purposes of clarity in scientific procedure. I look at a barometer and I say that it will probably rain tomorrow. This judgment, von Meinong and others have insisted, has nothing to do with series or relative frequency. It is about tomorrow only. But, if looking at the barometer has any rational connection with the statement that it will probably rain tomorrow, it is because a certain state of the barometer is generally if not always followed by rain the next day. The probability that Mr. X will be re-elected is determined by our evidence, and the odds may vary, according to the number of factors we take into account; but he will be either re-elected or defeated according to the number of electoral votes, and when either happens, there will be no probability about it.

Considerations of this sort have served to strengthen the subjectivist interpretation of probability, to wit: that probability measures only our ignorance or our belief. This view is based on the popular confusion between subjectivity and relativity, on the failure to take account of objective relativity. Without dwelling on this point we may note that the subjectivist theory of probability does not remove any difficulty and creates new ones. If probability is a measure of our ignorance, how can physical science and practical management of a business like insurance be based on it? Besides, is it true that degrees of belief can be measured with the degree of refinement which a mathematical theory of probability involves? *It is not the fact that we believe, or how intensely we believe, that determines probability, but the content of what is asserted.* The probability of an event is relative to the evidential facts in its favor; and that is why the same event may have different degrees of probability in different contexts, just as any given line may subtend different angles. There is therefore nothing really paradoxical in the difficulty emphasized by Bertrand and Poincaré that the probability of a random chord being greater than the side of an inscribed triangle has one value if we start with one hypothesis, and another value if we start with a different hypothesis.

The foregoing analysis of probability has emphasized the rational rigor of the relative frequency theory as contrasted with other theories of probability which are prevalent in the field of philosophy. In the course of examination, several objections to this view of probability may be scrutinized.

On the frequency theory every statement about the probability of a single event can be interpreted only as an elliptic statement about the relation between classes of events. Against this it is urged that we all do make statements about the probability of single events which seem to us significant before any of us hear of the frequency theory. Frequency, it is urged, is certainly not what we mean when we say that a certain individual is probably guilty, that a certain person from whom we have not heard for a long time is probably dead, or that there is probably some lurking fallacy in an argument which proceeds from self-evident premises to an unwelcome conclusion.

Against this argument we must insist on the distinction between logical implication and what it is that people are conscious of when they use certain words. What people actually have in mind when they talk about causality, or a debt of thirty billion dollars, or the electron theory of matter, are most diverse and altogether irrelevant for a scientific theory as to the meaning of these concepts. For a scientific theory, the meaning of these concepts can only consist of the definitive propositions in which such concepts are employed. It is well known that our ordinary consciousness of meaning is incomplete. We have in mind only an image, picture or symbol, visible or audible, of the subject matter about which we make assertions. But into this psychologic inquiry we need not enter at all. For purposes of physical theory, rest and motion are meaningless except in relation to some body or system of reference; and any one of us may be at rest with reference to this chair but in motion with reference to the earth or the sun. Without the addition of such reference, the notions of rest or motion seem to have a meaning, but are in fact incomplete symbols and do not denote anything definite. Thus probability is relative. It is meaningless to speak of the probability of a single event taken in isolation. If I say that the probability of a die not falling on the side marked 3 is ⅚, that ratio is clearly not a characteristic of the actual event by itself. The actual die will either fall on that side or not. The ⅚ describes not the actual single event as it occurs but the relative frequency with which events of this kind occur in our assumed universe.

Now, it may be urged that when we speak of the probability of unique events, we do not think of classes of events, but of the individual case. But what does it mean to think of an individual case? If our thought is rational it seeks reason or evidence for the given event. If we find any reason or evidence, its force will apply to an indefinite number of instances similar to ours. If I reason that Mr. Morgan is a patriot because all bankers are, the force of the argument does not depend upon the peculiarity of Mr. Morgan. I can replace Morgan with Baker or any other individual. Any X is a Z, if all X's are Y's and all Y's are Z's. The rational force while felt in a single case cannot be restricted to it. There is, therefore, nothing strange in saying that while we speak of the probability of single events, the logical or rational force of our statement has to do with certain features of it which are essentially repeatable. The unrepeatable individual, indeed, is not the object of science and certainly cannot be expressed in language.

Another objection to the frequency theory is that it requires the concept of the long run, which is not applicable to unique or historical events. This objection has merit only if the term "long run" suggests an actual series of repetitions, but that is hardly necessary for the frequency theory. All that is necessary for our purpose is that the elements of our problem shall be capable of *possible* repetition, and this is involved in any rational analysis.

The unfortunate introduction of the word "limit" in the frequency theory, by Cournot and others, has led to a host of objections against the relative frequency theory of probability. It may be stated categorically, however, that the technical concept of limit as applied by mathematicians is not necessary for our purpose. A mathematical limit is characteristic of a convergent series whose law is definite. The series to which probability applies need not have that characteristic. For the concept of probability we do not need to know the law of the series. In fact, we often apply probability to a series that we know only empirically without any indication of its definitive character beyond the terms examined. The terms may vary around a mode or median and for many purposes we may regard the variations as negligible. When we say that the readings vary between certain limits, we mean, then, to use the word *limit* in the popular sense of extremes of variation (or end terms).

Stated positively, this means that when we observe the fall of a penny a large number of times, we generally start with the hypothesis that one side will turn up as frequently as the other. Rarely, if ever, do we see this actually embodied. It certainly cannot be embodied in an odd number of throws, yet we are convinced that any deviation in favor of one side will sooner or later be balanced by a deviation on the other side.

And unless the evidence of the actual throws is overwhelming against our hypothesis, we are satisfied to neglect the deviations.

In what sense can the frequency theory be applied to the determining of the probability of a theory? It has been objected that the relative frequency with which the consequences of a theory are true is a concept that cannot be used at all. If, for example, every fifth proposition deducible from a given theory turned out to be false, we should not say that the probability of the theory being true is $\frac{4}{5}$. We should rather say that the theory is false, if even one of a thousand of its consequences is false. There is, however, no inconsistency between denying that an inference always follows, and asserting that the inference will give us a certain frequency of materially true conclusions. The statement that a theory is true is the statement that all its consequences are true, and therefore is logically contradicted by the proposition that one of its consequences is false. But the probability that conclusions from a given theory will be true, even when the theory is not absolutely true itself, is an entirely different matter. For a theory which, though not entirely true, is an approximation of the truth, may give us true conclusions within certain limits or in a certain proportion of cases. Accordingly, in the suggested case in which every fifth conclusion of a given theory is false, we should say there is enough evidence to prove the theory absolutely false as a universal proposition, though we can deduce probable consequences from it, in the sense that a prediction that a given consequence has the trait which the theory postulates will in general be true four times out of five.

The most serious objection that Keynes offers against the frequency theory is that it does not explain the probability of analogy, induction or generalization. Granted that our statistical information shows that in the past, three out of ten children died within the first four years of their lives, how can that explain the probability of the inference that this ratio will prevail? There is no difficulty here at all. The generalization in question is surely not always justified. Very often such generalizations are found to be misleading because the conditions under which past observations were made may no longer prevail. Dialectically, we could say that if the conditions which made the thing true in the past continued to exist, the same ratio would prevail, but that is not the inference or categoric conclusion in question. That conclusion obviously will be true in some cases and not in others according to the way in which we select our material. It is, therefore, according to our analysis a probable inference, and the strength of its probability depends on the kind of evidence we have that the same conditions will hold.

The frequency theory seems to emphasize number and to ignore the quality of events or propositions. Hence, it is urged that relative frequency is, at best, only a consequence of the quality or the rational force of what we know in relation to the proposition considered, and that this quality or rational force is not dependent upon relative frequency.

This objection would be sound if relative frequency and rational force of arguments were mutually exclusive. But the frequency theory does not need to deny the rational force which arguments have to a mind that is trained to weigh evidence. The question is, whether this weight of evidence is something mystical and unanalyzable, or whether it can be shown to involve something verifiable, and the theory of relative frequency does give us something verifiable.

It has been argued that we often consider the probability of a proposition with respect to an hypothesis contrary to all the known facts. How can we possibly introduce relative frequencies in such a case? The answer is, that an hypothesis, if it is significant, defines a possible universe, and in that universe there are classes of possible objects in which certain sub-classes can have relations to the species or genera of which they are part. Indeed, all theoretic science which follows from such laws as the law of the lever, the law of falling bodies *in vacuo,* the laws of thermo-dynamics, all describe what would happen in a possible universe not actually attainable on earth. These laws serve as principles according to which actual things can be judged to be more or less in conformity or approximation.

It must be admitted that Keynes is right in raising the objection that not all probability judgments have a definite numerical value, and if the frequency theory assumed that they always do that would be a fatal objection. For not only is the assignment of numerical values to probable judgments generally impossible but we very often assert probability as the antithesis of certainty in instances where we have no numerical comparison of any sort. This contention is perfectly true, but it confuses the evidence for the judgment with the content of the judgment. In other words, we can make an estimate or guess as to relative frequency without having any evidence to determine its precise value. In any case, it is not necessary to assume that all probability judgments do have a definite numerical value. It is sufficient to grant, as we must, that some judgments founded on statistical evidence do have ascertainable probability values, and other judgments of probability can frequently be correlated with such statistical evidence. I confess this seems a *tour de force*, but I think the extent of statistical evidence is capable of considerable enlargement. At any rate, statistical evidence, as I think even Keynes admits, fits in with the frequency theory better than with any other theory that has thus far been developed,—which is as much as can be said for any scientific hypothesis.

Finally, it is urged that when we apply a general rule to an individual case we have, at best, only a probability that the individual case does conform to the general rule, and that this probability cannot be explained on the frequency theory. The true force of this objection can be seen if we realize that it holds of all deductive arguments. If I say that all electrified bodies repel each other, this is an electrified body, etc., the judgment as to this body is a *salte mortale*. It rests upon evidence which can never be conclusive. Now, the probability of a premise does not affect the certainty of the inference, though it does affect the conclusion.

Most of the objections to the relative frequency theory of

probability are significant only if we ignore the context and ground of scientific knowledge. Otherwise, the only alternative is to accept the frequency theory as the best exemplification of what we mean by probability.

To accept the frequency theory in these terms is not to deny the legitimacy of other interpretations of probability. For it must be admitted that relative frequency is not the only test of probability. Granted that the absolute number of instances of a given proposition is decisive for the weight of argument in support of the proposition, it remains true that some arguments carry greater weight than others because their experimental bases are more carefully constructed or generally more reliable for some other reason. And while this greater reliability does not appear to be a question of mere numbers, it may be reduced to a question of the comprehensiveness of an inquiry or experiment, which is a relevant factor under the relative frequency theory. We may put this in another way by saying that when we eliminate disturbing conditions, or conditions irrelevant to the problem under consideration, we increase the scope of applicability of the observed result and thus in a measure increase its numerical applicability.

2. *Probability and Pure Mathematics*

The significant work of mathematicians on the theory of probability has given rise to the popular misimpression that probability is a purely mathematical concept. This misimpression is somewhat aided by the fact that where popular usage refers to something as possible but not probable, the mathematician speaks of a probability less than half. This seems to identify the mathematically probable with the possible and indeed few mathematical treatises clearly distinguish between these two concepts. Thus mathematicians often put such problems as, "What is the probability of a die falling once in two throws on a given side?", as if the fact that there are six possibilities in each throw is sufficient to determine the answer. That, however, is clearly not the case. For unless these possibilities are equally probable, there is no way by which the given answer can be logically proved. And it is not true that all possibilities are equally probable. A die may fall on the side marked five or it may not. Are these two possibilities equally probable? Certainly not, unless the die is especially loaded—and that is a physical fact and not one of pure mathematics. Something more than a number of abstract possibilities is needed to determine probability and that is the assumption that various possibilities are equally probable, and there is no way by which this can be defined in verifiable terms except as a prediction of what will actually happen under certain conditions, i.e., the frequency with which the given side will occur in an indefinitely long series of throws. If dice are physical objects and their throws are physical events, any prediction in regard to them must assume physical knowledge over and above purely mathematical considerations. The mathematician can assume a certain number of possibilities to be equally probable and draw necessary conclusions as to the permutations and combinations of such events. His reasoning will be purely mathematical so long as he is reasoning from certain numerical assumptions to their necessary consequences. But the subject matter about which he reasons has a physical aspect, and the theorems of mathematical probability are applicable to the physical world only if we make certain assumptions as to physical states. It would therefore make for clarity of thought if all mathematical problems were to state explicitly what events or combinations are assumed as equiprobable. Without such an assumption, no mathematical computation of probability is possible.

3. *Probability and Ethics*

Our analysis of probability shows that it is always a question of more or less. In conduct, however, we must decide categorically—yes or no. This necessity for definitive choice, coupled with the traditional and organic fear of departing from the beaten path, feeds the feeling of absolute moral certainty. It will not satisfy the traditionalist to say that bigamy, lying and murder are generally evil in their consequences. For this opens the road to reflection. Are there not cases where these things are justified? And if so, under what conditions will they obtain? Traditional moralists with a penchant for the authority of the prophet or pedagogue, therefore, lay down absolute rules: Thou shalt not commit adultery; Thou shalt not lie; Thou shalt not kill. And Kant rightly insisted that such absolute commands cannot be based upon experience, for experience can give us only probabilities and a judgment of probability cannot carry absolute authority.

Suppose, however, that we conceive of the rules of morality as Aristotle does, as the rules of wisdom for the attainment of the good in life, like the rules of hygiene or the directions of any artist to those who wish to follow him in the attainment of beauty. Such rules cannot be freed from considerations of probability, but they are, therefore, no more to be despised than the advice of a doctor or expert engineer. In any case, we must recognize that what is our duty in any given situation involves a factual judgment, that in this situation, certain physical circumstances are to be found which cannot be dissociated from their probable consequences. This is obviously the case in the field of social ethics where we discuss the right and the wrong of policies on the tacit assumption that these policies will probably have certain consequences. But the absolutists, here and elsewhere, are not altogether wrong. They rightly protest against the positivists who would deduce what we *ought* to do from premises which contain assertions only about what is, a procedure which is ethically confusing and logically impossible. Some assumption as to what is good or desirable or what we ought to do, we cannot avoid, and the question of the consistency of judgments, in this respect, is a question of logic and invariant relations. But it is very doubtful whether the ideal of logical consistency of our judgment excludes the possibility of diverse ethical systems, equally valid under diverse conditions. Specific ethical judgments involve all sorts of assumptions and cannot be more than probable.

Probabilism in ethics has received a bad name since Pascal's famous *Lettres Provincales*, and the prestige of the Kantian ethics as well as of Scotch intuitionalism has added to this impression. Nevertheless, we can admit that our actual judgments of right and wrong can at best claim only a high degree of probability, and it would be well if we recognized this more universally. For to believe that ethical judgments are absolute is to become indifferent to doubts in regard to them, and thus to encourage the many unconscionable and cruel prejudices which history shows to have paraded as moral imperatives throughout the ages. If our moral judgments rest on experience and can only attain a higher degree of probability, then it is up to us to do our utmost to examine the facts carefully and to attain the highest degree of probability that is humanly possible.

4. *Probability and Metaphysics*

It is curious to note that in the realm of religion and metaphysics, where prevail the greatest differences of opinion, almost all parties are agreed in rejecting the notion that knowledge in these matters might be only probable. But it is obvious that our knowledge of the absolute totality of things or of an omniscient and benevolent Creator, whose nature is beyond our powers of imagination, cannot be demonstrable knowledge, in the ordinary sense of knowledge and proof. The various proofs for the existence of God rest upon principles which appeal to certain minds, but which others can question without disbelieving in logic. The modern tendency to question self-evident principles can certainly not be excluded from these realms. But the reflective mind cannot stop with so-called empirical knowledge, for the more we reflect, the more uncertain become the assumptions on which our empirical judgments rest. The drive to consider that which is beyond the merely actual is at the basis not only of all human activity but of all effort to understand. In that sense metaphysics is not an additional realm, but something implicit in all rational endeavor. Traditional metaphysics thought that if it could find something permanent and self-evident it would have the key for the understanding of the totality of the world. Modern reflection is not certain that any such key is to be found, and it is highly skeptical as to whether we can treat of the totality of things under the same categories as we treat other objects of rational consideration. Constructive metaphysics as an imaginative anticipation of what the growth of knowledge may reveal will always be with us, but the results will always move in the realm of the more or less probable rather than the absolutely true or the absolutely false. And yet, the traditional attitude is not entirely to be discarded, for in concatenating our probabilities we must rely on logical or mathematical considerations which are themselves not probable but invariant.

What kind of a world is it of which judgments of probability can be validly asserted? For if the mind includes everything, the statement that probability exists in the mind only is meaningless, and if there is some reality other than the mind to which its ideas must point or conform, then the question remains as to what earthly or unearthly relation ideas can have to a world which is radically different from them.

If probability is a genuine trait of the world in which we live, the latter contains many objects, patterns, configurations, or abstract aspects which are indefinitely repeatable in certain ratios or proportions, and this means a world in which not all things are possible, but some things are impossible. If the actual world is thus a selection from a number of possible ones, actual objects could have been arranged in different ways without ceasing to be intelligible. And this means that there is, in the world, an element of contingency which is radically undetermined. We have noted elsewhere the error implied in the common assumption that the reign of law, such as physical science proclaims, requires absolute determinism. On the contrary, if there is a genuine plurality of atoms, electrons or any other units which determine each other according to invariant relations, there must be, by the very hypothesis, some distinction between the existence of any one thing and the influences which operate upon it. We cannot believe in a world of functions without anything which functions, in grins without cats. Ultimately, the world is what it is, and logical necessity can only be the derivative from certain characters which happen to exist or to be. Contingency can never be eliminated, no matter how general law may be. The attempt to derive existence from concepts is doomed, not only in the theologic, but in other realms. The world is more than relations of order, though, of course, it is vain to attempt to describe that which is beyond all relations and predicates. Surely, no description of what we are can be exact and completely exhaustive of our actual being, and this must be true of any world in which there is a genuine plurality. The philosopher must seek to find as much as he can without suffering the illusion of complete attainment. To that end, reflection on the nature of probability is most helpful.

VII

The Statistical View of Nature [1]

Since the beginning of modern statistical science, its leaders such as Quetelet have in agreement with the pioneers of the other social sciences insisted that progress is possible only if we introduce the rigorous and deterministic methods which have brought such great success to the physical sciences. And now we are witnessing physical science itself not only raising doubt as to the adequacy of Newtonian mechanics and the law of the conservation of energy, but also challenging the entire classical conception of physical causation. This has caused considerable disturbance in the social sciences; but certain philosophers, both positivists and those of theologic leaning, are rejoicing. For the latter have been asserting for some time that our knowledge of physics is statistical only, of the same kind as our knowledge of social phenomena when these are the result of large numbers.

We can perhaps most profitably approach this issue if we begin by considering the characteristics of statistical knowledge, and then try to analyze the nature of statistical mechanics and the significance of determinism in a statistical view of the world. Analysis along this course may suggest some application as to the limitations of statistical measurement.

At the outset of our inquiry it is interesting to note how many fundamental terms which the social sciences are trying to adopt

[1] Read before the Ninety-seventh Annual Meeting of the American Statistical Association, New York City, December 28, 1935. Published in *Journal of the American Statistical Association*, June, 1936, vol. 33, pp. 327-347.

from physics have as a matter of historical fact originated in the social field. Take, for instance, the notion of *cause*. The Greek αἰτία or the Latin *causa* was originally a purely legal term. It was taken over into physics, developed there, and in the eighteenth century brought back as a foreign-born king for the adoration of the social sciences. The same is true of the concept of *law of nature*. Originally a strictly anthropomorphic conception, it was gradually depersonalized or dehumanized in the natural sciences and then taken over by the social sciences in an effort to eliminate final causes or purposes from the study of human affairs. It is therefore not anomalous to find similar transformations in the history of such fundamental concepts of statistics as *average* and *probability*. The concept of *average* was developed in the Rhodian laws as to the distribution of losses in maritime risks. After astronomers began to use it in correcting their observations it spread to other physical sciences; and the prestige which it thus acquired has given it vogue in the social field. The term *probability*, as its etymology indicates, originates in practical and legal considerations of probing and proving. And now we are trying to fit social phenomena into the patterns of probability worked out by mathematical physicists such as LaPlace and Poisson, and by mathematicians like Gauss and Karl Pearson.

1. *The Nature of Statistical Knowledge*

What are the essential traits that differentiate statistical from other kinds of knowledge? It is usual to discriminate it from history on the one hand and from mechanics on the other.[2] These distinctions are worth noting.

Historical knowledge is concerned with individual objects or events, with individual persons, nations, or institutions having a

[2] The reader will note that the text distinguishes between different kinds of *knowledge*. The scientific statistician, of course, must use all the kinds of knowledge he can obtain, including pure mathematics, which is certainly not in itself statistical.

definite date or position in time. Statistical knowledge differs in this respect by being concerned with numerical relations in multitudes which are fungible, i.e., in which individual differences are ignored. To know that the population of the United States in 1800 was 4,000,000 is, to be sure, historical in so far as it describes the United States at that time and indicates its power relative to other nations, but it is statistical in respect to the individuals who constitute that population. It gives us no information about any one of them. And this ignorance is not cured by averaging. If I am told that the average family then consisted of 5.6 persons, I do not thereby learn anything about any actual family. We are not thus denying that statistical information is a necessary aid in the understanding of history. To determine what was the population of Athens in 430 B.C. or of the United States in 1790 is surely a most significant task of history; but we do not thereby attain direct information about any individual citizen, e.g., what the peculiar traits were that made some of them, like Pericles or Washington, such outstanding figures. This distinction between the historical and the statistical is also valid in the realm of physics. If I know that there was an earthquake or an eclipse of the moon or that a column of mercury attained a certain height on a given occasion, my knowledge is so far purely historical. And from a logical point of view our knowledge of the geologic changes which our earth has undergone is of the same logical pattern as our knowledge of the changes in the dynasties which have ruled Egypt. In both cases we reconstruct individual past events on the basis of observations of presently existing records or remains. On the other hand, our knowledge of physical nature is strictly statistical whenever it is concerned with averages such as heights or weights of groups of objects or with the relative frequencies with which certain phenomena occur.

The distinction between statistical and mechanical knowledge deserves even greater attention. The classical view held generally throughout the eighteenth and nineteenth centuries regarded the principles of Newtonian mechanics, like those of

Euclidean geometry, as self-evident or in some way necessary. Thus, philosophers like Kant, Whewell, and Wundt have tried to derive the Newtonian laws of mechanics from entirely *a priori* considerations. Also, great physicists like J. J. Thomson, the successor of Maxwell, explicitly declared the laws of dynamics to be in some sense superior to those which, like the second law of thermodynamics, are merely based on experience. But the general distrust of self-evident principles that has come with non-Euclidean geometry and the recent development of non-Newtonian mechanics makes this position a difficult one to maintain. All the ultimate laws of nature which we know are contingent, that is, we know of no reason why these laws should prevail in fact rather than others which are conceivable; and the really decisive evidence for the truth of the laws of any mechanical system is that their consequences are verifiable, that is, agree with experimental observations. Yet though mechanical laws of the classical type are not justified by their self-evidence and are not independent of experience, they can be clearly distinguished from statistical laws by the fact that they *assert universal or invariant connections in nature*. Whenever we have two particles, they attract each other with a force that varies inversely as the square of the distance between them; or, whenever a body moves freely under the influence of a constant force, the velocity acquired will be proportional to the time during which the force acts. A single exception can thus logically refute the law.

Now, statistical laws or correlations do not take such universal form, but assert rather certain frequencies, for example, that a little over 51 per cent of all births are male. This, however, does not enable us to predict individual instances. To say that 75 per cent of the Romans were tall, e.g., above 5'5", gives us no warrant for inferring that Cato was tall. And to say that this information makes it probable that Cato was tall does not really determine the individual case, for he may well have been only 5'4" despite the fact that so many of his fellow-countrymen were taller. This makes a tremendous difference in the problem of verification. A universal proposition asserts something to be impossible, and if that which is thus excluded does take place our proposition is definitely refuted. It is thus always conceivable and sometimes actually the case that a single crucial experiment can refute an hypothesis or supposed law. And if another hypothesis is thus confirmed, the latter may be said to be verified in the sense that it has been shown to be in greater harmony with experimental observation than its rival or competing hypothesis. Thus, if the classical theory predicts an observable motion relative to the ether, and such motion does not show itself under proper conditions of observation in the Michelson-Morley experiment, we have definite evidence against the classical theory. And if the Einstein theory of relativity can explain this experiment as well as all that the classical theory does, we have definite reasons for preferring it. Statistical generalizations, however, cannot be so readily verified by any crucial experiment. Consider, for instance, the well-established statistical observation that as the number of voters increases, the pluralities in favor of some candidate increase also. According to this view, there is a negligible probability that the millions of voters of New York State will in the next election be exactly evenly divided between the Democratic and Republican candidates for Governor. If, however, that should actually happen, it will not refute our statistical generalization since the latter does not declare a tie vote under these conditions to be impossible.

It may well be objected that this sharp distinction between mechanical and statistical laws in regard to verification, overlooks the fact that statistical laws apply not to individual instances but only to large groups or over a long run, and that when so taken they are verifiable. Thus, consider the classical statistical law referred to before as to the ratio of male to female births. If, for a long period and over a wide area, this ratio is not found to prevail, we should surely regard it as refuted by experience, and some other ratio might be verified. This objection, however, while perfectly true does not fully obviate the difficulty to which we have pointed. For the test as to when a run is sufficiently long to verify a statistical law cannot in the nature of the case be very precise. A few repetitions of the Michelson-Morley experiment are necessary to make certain that we have not overlooked something. But they are repetitions of what is essentially the same experiment which if true is sufficient to overthrow the contradictory universal. But it is difficult to determine just how many reports of different cities for different years would be necessary to refute a statistical theory as to the proportion of male and female births.

I do not wish to ignore difficulties in pressing the foregoing point. The history of science undoubtedly shows that crucial experiments are very infrequent, and that they do not play the absolutely decisive role which popular histories of science ascribe to them. No single experiment overthrew the Ptolemaic astronomy. Despite Lavoisier's experiments, the phlogiston theory continued to be held for a long time. Nevertheless, the issues in each of these cases were definitely formulated because universal laws were involved and single facts, such as the observed phases of the planet Venus or the increased weight of certain substances after being burned, were definitely and directly contrary to the predictions. If a single fact is not generally sufficient to overthrow completely a supposed universal law which it contradicts, it is because an established hypothesis generally rests not on a single chain of arguments but on many interwoven threads, so that the cutting of one of those threads is not at once fatal. Moreover, theories are flexible and can be reformulated, or have auxiliary hypotheses added, e.g., Lavoisier's experiments can be explained by endowing phlogiston with negative weight. But in any case every single theoretic statement in regard to nature takes the form of universal propositions which can be definitely refuted by a single contradictory instance, and this is not true of statistical statements.

Another way of stating the distinction between mechanical and statistical laws is that the former state causal relations while the latter are mere correlations. It is not necessary to go into the traditional discussions as to the nature of causality. It is sufficient for our present purpose to insist that a causal relation means some intimate connection or thread of identity between two things, traits or events thus connected, while a statistical correlation may mean nothing more than a temporary coincidence. The fallacious assumption that a high correlation must necessarily represent a causal relation, while not held by scientific statisticians, is still widely current. In a book of mine published some years ago, I referred to Dr. George Marshall who found a correlation of 87 per cent. between the membership of the International (really American) Machinists' Union and the death rate of the state of Hyderabad. Many of my readers have since protested vigorously that such a high correlation extending over twelve years cannot be accidental or devoid of real significance. But the fact is that the correlation does not hold beyond the period taken. Indeed, it obviously could not have prevailed before the Machinists' Union was formed when there was still a considerable death rate in the Hindu State. If more instances of this sort are not available it is because most of us have no interest in such purely logical demonstrations. We look for correlations where we suspect a real connection, and then we regard whatever small correlation we find as a proof of our hypothesis. Where there are genuine causal connections we should expect statistical correlation, but the converse is not necessarily true. Genuine physical and mechanical laws are thus more than statistical correlations. The law of the conservation of energy and Newton's law of motion are all empirical in the sense that they depend for their verification on observation, but they also indicate some element of identity in cause and effect, or antecedent and consequent, and that is more than mere statistical correlation. The observation that a certain correlation prevails for a certain period does not of itself give us reason for supposing that it prevailed before we observed it or that it will do so in the future. But scientific procedure in physics cannot go on without assuming that the relations we deal with prevailed before we discovered them and are independent of our knowing them. Careful statisticians recognize this when they draw a distinction between gross and refined statistics, between birth rates where the denominator is the total population and those based on the number of married women of child-bearing age. Such distinctions are based on the recognition that causal relations are necessary to give statistical correlations real significance.

The foregoing reflections suggest one of the reasons why there is in fact much less consensus in regard to social than in regard to physical laws as statements of invariant or causal relations. If we formulate a theory of business cycles or of the variations of the stock market, and the actual facts do not conform, we do not generally abandon the theory, but we explain the departure of the facts by means of disturbing factors that prevent a fair test of our assumed law. Now, the existence of perturbations is also found in physics. But in the latter the effect of disturbing forces can generally be measured independently. That, however, is generally impossible when, as in the case of the weather or of biologic and social phenomena generally, we have a large number of factors that are not independent of each other. Hence, in dealing with such complex phenomena we can seldom prove that if a given disturbing factor were absent, our assumed law would operate. To attain invariant relations we must be able to isolate our factors or vary one at a time. Otherwise, we have too many variables and no assumption of ours can be definitely verified. The analysis of any situation into its related factors is therefore the condition for any definite test as to the truth of even statistical generalizations.

It is important to remember that we do not always get nearer to the truth by increasing the number of cases on which our generalization is based. Observations on fifty Chinese laundrymen no more justify a generalization as to Chinese in general than an observation of twenty Chinese, if they all come from Canton, all belong to the same society, etc. It is only when by good fortune the randomness of our samples does eliminate the fallacy of selection that a larger number gives better evidence than a smaller number. In the end, the truth of a generalization from a sample depends on the homogeneity of the group with respect to which we wish to generalize. A single experiment on a new substance, to test whether it is acid or alkaline, is much more convincing than the result of a questionnaire addressed to millions of army men to measure their intelligence. For the latter is not a simple quality of a uniformly repeatable pattern. In this respect the methods of social statistics are gross compared with refined analysis, so that when our analysis is thoroughgoing, as it generally is in physics, one or two samples are as good as a million. If what we are measuring is really homogeneous, one instance is sufficient. In the social field, therefore, statistics cannot take the place of analysis; and in fact acute social analysts have contributed much more to our understanding of social phenomena than those who, without genius or vision, have believed that the mere accumulation of instances will give us adequate knowledge.

Statistical method has been closely associated with the belief in what is loosely called induction, and it is often asserted that the founders of statistical science were men who, like Sir William Petty and those who organized the Royal Society, were influenced by Francis Bacon. It would take me far afield to show the mythical character of this history. A few observations, however, are essential. There can be no doubt that statistics deals with actuality, and that knowledge of actualities is always empirical, i.e., that we cannot obtain knowledge of existence by purely *a priori* methods. There is, however, no genuine progress in scientific insight through the Baconian method of accumulating empirical facts without hypotheses or anticipation of nature. Without some guiding idea we do not know what facts to gather. Without something to prove, we cannot determine what is relevant and what is irrelevant.

If we wish to find the laws of the weather, the thousands of millions of observations will not of themselves indicate the true causes of such phenomena. Only when we strike some fruitful idea or hypothesis such as the late Carl Barus did in determining the influence of dust on the concentration of moisture, can we make some progress in the understanding of nature. Economic statistics, charts of the variations of prices, incomes, imports and exports, etc., do not constitute science unless organized, controlled and informed by some general idea. A collection of data will not give us science any more than a collection of ores will give us metal works. We need fire to fuse our material into some pattern. In science we achieve that, if we discover the proper perspective from which the order of phenomena becomes visible to the trained eye.

This does not mean that we do not often go wrong because of false hypotheses, but it is well to recall the caution of a great naturalist, *viz.*, Charles Darwin, who rightly maintained that the danger of false hypotheses is never as great as that of a false observation. For even a false hypothesis may enable us to advance the organization of our material; but everything that is based on a false observation has to be undone before we can build anew on more reliable data. But note that even in statistical work we do not dispense with *a priori* assumptions, that is, with assumptions which are based on general considerations and which cannot be readily refuted by purely empirical data. We can see this in our various assumptions as to what are independent or equiprobable events. I do not wish to touch here on the subject of probability. But I must call attention to the fact that in all statistical measurement and inference we do involve ourselves in assumptions as to what events are equally probable and what events are independent. And in this field *a priori* considerations are most potent.

Ask people at large, What is the probability of a penny falling head? Almost everybody answers one-half, although few have ever taken an actual count of the relative frequency with which pennies fall head or tail. The answer comes in fact not on the basis of actual observation, but on the indetermination which prevents us from giving heads a preference over tails.[3] If, however, we ask whether Americans are as likely to pay their bills as Germans, we do not ask for data, nor are we likely to say that

[3] See *supra*, pp. 111-114.

one is as likely as the other. The answer will largely depend on where we live. Our belief, then, in the probability of an event is largely determined by considerations other than statistical study.

We must, therefore, reject the tradition of which Quetelet and Buckle were the high priests, and which spoke of statistical averages as if they were iron and unchangeable laws of nature beyond human control. (People still speak of the average or the mean about which our numbers oscillate, e.g., as the normal man, with some implication perhaps that the normal is the perfect.) Obviously there is no law of nature which compels the normal family to have 2.7 children or the normal man to divorce his wife or commit bankruptcy once in so many years. There is, therefore, also no merit in the argument that the existence of such averages proves that human volition cannot change what these averages describe. Statistical averages do give us knowledge of groups if there are in fact laws which keep the distribution in those groups approximately stable. But that empirical generalizations do not always give us genuine laws can be seen in popular generalizations about diet, exercise, the evil eye, lucky and unlucky numbers, the length of cycles on the stock market, etc. Are such generalizations more reliable if expressed in numbers, charts or curves?

As a matter of fact we know of no statistical laws comparable in constancy with the law of multiple proportion in chemistry or of planetary motion in astronomy. All the social statistical averages that we know vary somewhat, as Lexis and others have shown, from year to year and are conditioned by our social and political regulations. Many of them, e.g., the number of bank failures per annum, or of car loadings or automobile accidents, have no meaning except under special conditions which come and pass, while mechanical laws are independent of geography and chronology. For the very meaning of causality is that mere position in time or place cannot in itself determine a natural change.

Suppose that in the social field you find a formula like Pareto's that fits the tables of incomes for several countries for a number of years. Does it follow that it is a law which will persist and which legislation cannot change? Some have actually argued to that effect, but in point of fact it is not true universally, and does not hold for small incomes.[4]

Statistical information needs refined analysis before it can lead to causal or rigorously scientific information. If we know that the average life of men is less than that of women we ask, is it due to occupation, to habits, or to organic handicaps? We need to pass from the macroscopic to the microscopic point of view.

It is necessary to insist on these obvious reflections because of the widespread manner of speaking of the law of large numbers and the normal frequency curve as if they were *a priori* laws of nature governing the distribution of all possible phenomena. This popular view is logically groundless and vitiates much statistical work such as that involved in much of our intelligence testing.

Let us remember that the curve of distribution derived from the Gaussian assumptions can hold true only where these assumptions happen to be true in fact. Now, the curve assumes that our phenomena or instances are symmetrically distributed, but this is obviously not true of all phenomena even if their number is indefinitely increased. Many anthropologic measurements certainly do not conform to it, e.g., the death rate, the acceleration and retardation of growth in children, and the like. In many cases, to be sure, larger groups show greater stability and more balance or symmetry than the smaller groups which constitute them, but the reverse is also true at times. The normal probability curve is a help in analysis, but as a description of nature it is true only of those groups of figures which happen to con-

---

[4] The difference between an empirical and a rational formula can be seen when we compare the carpenters' rule for constructing a right angle with the Pythagorean theorem. The carpenters' rule holds only for lengths of 3, 4, and 5, while the Pythagorean theorem gives us a whole system of geometric propositions or an infinite series of such possible numbers.

form to it. There is no fair presumption that all groups will conform.

2. *Statistical Mechanics*

So far I have been considering the distinction between statistical laws or correlations on one hand and mechanical laws on the other.' But we have with us the science of statistical mechanics. What light does it throw on our issue? Let us consider it in three stages: first, the classical form of statistical mechanics; second, the modification introduced by the quantum theory; and third, the more recent wave mechanics and the Indeterminacy Principle.

The conception of a statistical knowledge of nature was first clearly enunciated by Maxwell (though partly anticipated by Clausius) in connection with the law of entropy. In his day it had been assumed that all genuine physical laws must be deducible from Newtonian mechanics. But the irreversibility of certain physical changes, e.g., the diffusion of gases or the fact that heat is conducted only from hotter to colder bodies, could not be deduced from mechanical principles concerning phenomena that are essentially reversible. This led Maxwell and Boltzmann to the idea that this irreversibility is not a fundamental law of nature holding like the laws of Newtonian mechanics always and everywhere from the largest mass to the smallest particle, but that it is a derivative result from the arrangement of molecular motions according to the curve of "error" or probability. From this point of view it is by no means impossible, though highly improbable, that some phenomena may actually take place contrary to the law of entropy. There have indeed been those who have urged that organic phenomena and even Brownian movements illustrate this possibility. It should be noted, however, that this classical system of so-called statistical mechanics does not proceed from empirical observations, by averaging and establishing correlations. Rather does it begin by assuming that there are definite laws which determine the distribution of molecular velocities in accordance with the Gaussian function originally derived to describe the distribution of errors of observation. This law of distribution is thus assumed to be an invariant law of nature, though it does not enable us to determine the position of any particular molecule. It is well to note also that statistical mechanics is still mechanics. It continues to assume the Hamiltonian principle, and still proceeds from a theoretically assumed system of mechanical laws in the microscopic realm to explain observable macroscopic phenomena. No wonder, therefore, that Maxwell could talk of statistical mechanics and yet believe in the absolute uniformity of all molecules, fresh as they issued from the hand of the Creator.

At the end of the 19th century, its leading physicist, the venerable Lord Kelvin, spoke of two clouds in the mechanical view of the universe,—its difficulties in explaining the Michelson-Morley experiment and the partition of energy in the spectrum. Both of these difficulties proved insurmountable and led to revolutionary changes. The first difficulty led to the non-Newtonian mechanics of Einstein's relativity theory. The second difficulty led to the perhaps more radical departure from classical mechanics, the quantum theory of Planck and Einstein. The classical theory regarded the universe as made up ultimately of separate particles, and yet the radiation of energy was regarded as continuous—a view which Einstein has well characterized as maintaining that the world is both soup and a bag of hard peas. Now, the actual distribution of energy in the spectrum cannot be fitted into the theory that energy radiation is continuous, and this seems to eliminate the continuity of the world which is essential to the classical geometric view that goes back through Newton, Galileo and Kepler to the early Greek geometers. The world consists not only of individual particles but also of multitudes of quanta of energy. This strengthens the statistical view so far as the latter proceeds by summation. The quantum theory, however, not only retains mechanical or invariant laws, such as are embodied in Hamilton's Principle, but adds new ones, to wit: exclusion principles such as Pauli's, which assert that certain states are impossible in nature.

After a series of great achievements, the quantum theory began to encounter insurmountable difficulties and a seemingly more revolutionary form of mechanics—popularly known as wave mechanics—began to take possession of the field. The suggestion of the more recent quantum mechanics that not only electrons but even material particles are waves seems to bring us back to the categories of continuity, but such waves must not be taken literally as similar to the waves of a string or of a body of water. The "wave" is merely a mathematical function which describes the probability or relative frequency with which an electron will be found in a given position. We need not go into the mathematics of the psi function, or ask in what sense it, multiplied by its conjugate, measures the amplitude of the wave. It is sufficient for our purpose that the fundamental equation of the unit of our microscopic cosmos takes the form not of a classical universal statement but of a probability function.

From the popular viewpoint, the most impressive novelty of this mechanics is Heisenberg's Indeterminacy Principle, according to which all physical measurements are subject to an indetermination within one quantum. We have always known empirically that our measurements vary and that laws or universal propositions about the physical universe can never be absolutely verified by actual measurements. Heisenberg's Principle, however, goes further and gives us a theoretic basis in the very nature of our mechanical laws for assigning a definite limit beyond which greater accuracy is unattainable. This in itself does not necessarily mean a denial of the principle of causality or an assertion of indeterminism in the objective physical world. It may be explained as a consequence of the fact that any measurement which involves observation of nature through light is itself a physical operation which disturbs the object observed. But be that as it may, the radical feature of the new mechanics is that its basic law or equation does not assert an invariant rule that determines the position and velocity of every individual particle, but asserts rather a probability function so that with regard to any electron or photon it can tell us only the relative frequency with which it will be found in a given position.

Though called the wave mechanics, the new physics really abandons the effort at a precise picture or mechanical model of what goes on in the microscopic realm that forms the physical sub-stratum of the visible world. It thus seems to abandon at the outset the possibility of an absolutely accurate and exhaustive description of the world. The indeterminacy which it introduces into physics is the indeterminacy of passing from an average or a probabality function to an individual instance. For a law which describes how a group of individuals are distributed does not give us precise knowledge of any individual constituent of the group. In this sense, the new mechanics is more conscious of the old truth that our most accurate knowledge of the physical world is never free from an element of probability.

While this involves profound technical transformations in physical science, it is not very revolutionary from the philosophic point of view. The new mechanics still operates with mathematical or invariant laws which relate one state of the physical system to past or future states. If any observable or macroscopic state of nature is determined, other states become determined. And that after all is the essence of the old mechanics. It was never necessary for physical science to assume that the classical mechanics completely exhausted the nature of things. The geometrical points and lines, the regular spheres, the perfectly rigid bodies of the classical mechanics were generally recognized as limiting concepts which represented, to be sure, features of the actual world but never exhaustive accounts. The new mechanics recognizes this limitation explicitly. It uses a wider conception of "co-ordinates" or the elements which determine a "state" of nature. Just as a number may be resolved in different ways as the products of two factors, or just as a force acting in any direction may be resolved into different pairs of components, so states of nature according to the new physics can be regarded as resolvable into different "superposed" states without altering the physical consequences. The invariant relations of mechanics bind features of the visible macroscopic states together, and in that respect the classic tradition of mechanics still holds the field, even though we no longer hold the faith in very *simple* laws governing all things from the greatest to the smallest.

If, instead of a simple statement, we have a probability theorem to verify, our problem becomes more difficult, but not impossible. For since probability to the statistician, at least, means relative frequency in a large group of numbers, a larger number of observations can show one probability theorem to be more in harmony with empirical observation than another. The point to note, then, is that Heisenberg's principle does not mean a lawless world. It means rather that the laws are of a different sort, the laws of the way in which multitudes are distributed rather than the way in which each particle behaves. We might venture to suggest that when the present excitement subsides, it will be found that the permanent results of the newer quantum mechanics confirm rather than overthrow the classical development in physics, just as the Einstein theory is now seen to be a development and completion of the Newtonian mechanics, saving its essence by modifying its formulae so that it can explain facts otherwise obdurate and intractable, such as the Michelson and Morley experiment. Indeed, what else should we expect, seeing that the new results have been obtained by the methods, instruments and assumptions of the classical mechanics?

3. *Statistics and Determinism*

Our brief glimpse of statistical mechanics reinforces the point that while statistical knowledge is distinct from mechanics it depends upon the latter as well as on history. There is no doubt that we can sometimes make progress in science by ignoring the question of mechanics and studying variations statistically. This has notably been the case with the Darwinian doctrine of natural selection. Neither Darwin nor Mendel went into the causes of variation. Still Mendel, trained as a mathematician and physicist, was able to find significant ratios which have advanced our knowledge of biologic phenomena. Two observations, however, must be made with regard to such progress. In the first place, such variations are within definite ranges and conform to recognizable patterns. There is no reason to suppose that if the variations were completely lawless, the resultant of a large number of them would show any order. If there be such a thing as the law of large numbers, it means that individual variations are governed by certain forces which bring about symmetry, decreasing frequencies of larger variations and all the other features which have to be assumed in order to deduce a frequency curve.

The second observation that we must make is that determination is relative to a system and therefore a matter of degree. "Who killed Cock Robin?" I may know definitely that it was done by an arrow and that may be enough for medical purposes. The moralist may not, however, find that sufficiently determinate. He may want to know who shot the arrow, and to this, the statement that it was done by a bird adds determination, for it excludes cats and hunters. It adds further determination to assert that it was done by a sparrow. But the law is not satisfied. It cannot proceed against all sparrows. It must determine which particular sparrow; and to draw up a valid indictment we must be able to specify where and when that fell deed was done. But even in this case we have a certain degree of indetermination. It might be sufficient to name the day, or within a few hours, whereas the deed itself could not have taken more than a few seconds. The fact is that while every event in nature is completely individualized, and every moment is different from every other, science is concerned with the fungible aspect of things, with those features which repeat themselves indefinitely.

The statistician used to be taught to have faith in determinism. Shall he now follow popularizers of recent physics and regard it as more scientific and up-to-date to profess indeterminism? It is tempting to say that he need take neither position, that all he needs to assume is that the universe has certain statistical regularities. What, however, does the latter statement imply? Admitting, for example, that we do not know the cause or causes which disintegrate any particular atom of uranium, and that all we do know are observable regularities in the behavior of the macroscopically visible masses, the fact remains that we cannot get along in science or in practice without expecting such regularities to recur. What ground have we for this expectation? The answer is that if we assume that our visible material is composed of an unimaginably large, but still calculable, number of invisible microscopic elements and that there are invariant laws according to which the happenings in this realm may be distributed and integrated, we have the most powerful means at our command for the discovery and understanding of an ever-increasing number of physical phenomena. We may therefore regard our assumption as being as well established or verified as any other bit of reliable knowledge in our possesson. If the most reliable social statistics, such as our mortality rates for different years, do not exhibit such measurable stability, it is not due merely to the smaller numbers in the latter field, but also to the fact that we have to deal in the social field with more factors that are not isolable, so that the invariant relations between them are not so readily ascertained. Hence more stable uniformities in the social realms are to be found not only by increasing the number of observations, but also by greater refinement of analysis. And this is exactly what a life insurance company does when instead of relying merely on an ever-larger number of death records, it takes advantage of medical research as to the *causes* which prolong or shorten life. Its business would be even more secure if it could determine the true causes of war and rebellion as well as earthquakes and plagues. Without causal laws for the recurrence of phenomena, all our observations would at best belong only to the field of history and not to natural science. We should put down in our books that these frequencies were observed at such and such times; but we should have no reason for expecting them to recur unless we believed such recurrence to be grounded in the nature of things.

A world of which statistical knowledge is possible is then a world in which there are variations which are in part individually unforeseeable and unpredictable, and therefore, inexplicable, but in which certain laws or regularities prevail. And if someone were to maintain, as Poincaré once suggested, that the laws of nature are themselves changing, then we should look for the law according to which such change takes place. A body changes its position according to some law which may be expressed as a constant velocity. So changes in velocity involve either a constant acceleration or one that changes according to some law of force. Ultimately all change involves some constancy. This is not empirical observation merely, but a condition of significant discourse. We cannot talk sense except on condition that our expressions have some definite meaning, and there is no meaning without some element of constancy in the field of variation, wherever that is chosen.

We may see the same truth in a more specifically statistical context. Traditional statistical procedure has always assumed that the variations in our measurements of such magnitudes as the height of a mountain or the specific gravity of iron, are not variations of the object itself, which is supposed to be constant, but are rather due to changes in our manipulations of the instruments of measurement. Now, suppose one questions this assumption, as Charles Peirce did long before the rise of the Indeterminacy Principle in physics. That highly original American philosopher ventured to suggest that behind the variations which fall within the limits of the error of measurement there are still smaller variations of the object itself, so that absolute constancy is an ideal never attained in actuality. As a philosophic suggestion this is worthy of more attention than we can devote to it here. For our present purpose it is sufficient to note that so long as the *variation can be expressed in some laws,* we have sufficient determinism for a statistical universe.

The recognition of the truth that constancy and variation are polar categories, opposed but inseparable, each meaningless apart from the other, enables us to deal more clearly with the vexed problem as to chance and determinism, neither of which can be eliminated from a statistical view of nature. It is popular to say that chance merely expresses our ignorance. But this offers no basis for mathematical computation. Measurable chance is something that certainly does not depend on *individual* ignorance. When I ask today what chance there is of my dying on a Tuesday, there is to be sure an element of ignorance involved; but that is the ignorance which is necessarily involved in any system of finite knowledge. Nothing that anyone can find out by medical research or otherwise will be sufficient to determine completely or absolutely the individual event—not even the fact that I am condemned by a court of law to be hanged on that day. But on the assumption that the day of the week makes no difference, that as many people die on Tuesdays as on any other day of the week, and that we have to die on one or another of these, the chance of its happening on a Tuesday is one-seventh. The ignorance involved here is not absolute. We do know something about the causes of death which enables us to be certain not only that death is coming, but that all pretensions that Tuesday is a lucky day or an unlucky one rest on insufficient evidence. If, on the other hand, it is a fact that people generally rest on Sunday or use their automobiles more, this may affect the relative death rates on the different days of the week. We may then say that a chance event dealt with in statistics is one for which we have determining principles that are necessary but insufficient. Pure chance is, indeed, incomprehensible unless defined with reference to some rule determining all possible variations. Thus, if we speak of the chances of a certain die turning up a six in three successive throws, we assume a limited number of possibilities all equally probable. If the chances were not regulated by some rule or order we should have no basis for any one result rather than any other. If there is any reason for any expectation, it is because there is some determination in the case, even though we do not know enough of what determines the individual event.

Similarly, reflection on the abstract character of the repeatable patterns which are the subject of statistical as well as of mechanical laws, enables us to see that law is meaningless apart from all contingency or chance.

It is a great mistake to believe that mechanical science involves a completely determined world, such as the Hegelian Absolute. On the contrary, if there are repeatable patterns or laws, there must be genuine plurality and this necessarily means relative independence or indifference. Thus, if everything depended on everything else, there would be no sense in saying that the photoelectric effect depends on the frequency of the impinging light, and not on other factors. Chance and determination are thus both objective logical consequences of the fact that any system with which science can deal must be defined and limited. Consider, for instance, the laws of celestial mechanics which make our solar system determinate. That some powerful body shall pass it so near as to cause it all to be smashed, would be an accident in the sense that from the co-ordinates of our system and the laws of celestial mechanics, the event cannot be determined. We can of course insist that if we knew the distance between our solar system and that body, and knew the rates at which they approach each other, we could predict the solar catastrophe. But this only means that we have to enlarge our original system to explain an event which would be an accident within the narrower domain. If, then, we distinguish between relativity and subjectivity, accidents are relative to the system and not to mere subjective opinions.

The question, however, may be raised: Are there any isolated systems? Are not all things inter-connected? In reply, we must insist that any intelligible system with which science can deal must be defined by a limited number of laws and determination thus limited. If you look at the world geometrically, certain features are connected with other features in certain invariant relations. If a disk, for instance, is circular or triangular, we compute its area according to certain invariant consequences of its geometric properties. That, however, which is necessary to determine an object geometrically will not be sufficient mechanically. So, likewise, the masses and motion of a system may not determine all of its physical properties, and the latter may not be sufficient to specify the properties of an organism. Similarly, biologic factors alone may not be sufficient to determine how a man will vote or respond to a given argument. In general, sciences aim to attain the form of logical systems in which a limited number of laws determine all the processes and connections between the variables in the field. The propositions of any science thus form what a mathematician calls a group. To the extent that a number of propositions can be derived from a certain number of assumptions, they are so far independent of the truth or falsity of other propositions.

The foregoing considerations do not deny that as science grows, we learn more about the determination of things. We can see this in the way science finds univocal relations to take the place of less determinate or one-to-many relations. Consider a case of what is called a plurality of causes. If I think of headaches as a single species, I may find the causes in eye-strain, in noxious smoke, in improper food, in the degeneration of certain tissues or some other factor. This may be sufficiently determinate for practical purposes. However, for scientific purposes I may analyze the different kinds of headaches and find that the one due to eye-strain is different from the one due to alcoholic drink. Or again, I may find that in all these different forms of headaches, there is one common factor, let us say a certain pressure on certain nerve endings. In the end, however, the determinism aimed at in any science is abstract. While events in nature are individualized, and every moment is different from every other, mechanical science and statistics are concerned with the fungible aspects of things, with those features which repeat themselves indefinitely. William James somewhere refers to an animal that is being experimented upon and referred to as a specimen, saying if it could, "Excuse me, it's me." We may stretch this and say that if the individual molecule could speak, it would say, "To be sure, I am a member of the noble species of hydrogen molecules, but I am altogether different from some of my degenerate neighbors." Physics may recognize different *kinds* of hydrogen atoms, just as vital statistics may distinguish between male and female deaths. It is to history and to intimate human relations that individual differences are of the utmost importance. The individual is more than any of its phases, and there would be no determination if there were not something to be determined. If, therefore, there is such a thing as genuine individuality, if the world consists of a number of things which are genuinely distinct from each other, although they modify each other in certain abstract ways, then there is a genuine incommensurability between the individual and the universal. Each is an unattainable limit to the other. No number of rules then can exhaustively determine the fullness of individual existence, though every change of abstract or isolated phase may be invariably connected with corresponding changes in other beings. Statistics and mechanics cannot therefore dispense with history.

4. *Statistics in the Social Sciences*

The foregoing reflections are not without bearing on the problem of measurement by statistical methods in the social sciences.

In the first place, we ought not to overlook the obvious distinction between enumeration and measurement. We can enumerate a multitude, but the measurement of a continuous quantity or magnitude involves other operations. Thus we measure length by laying off a standard unit. We measure weight by a process of balancing, and of course the measurement of all derivative magnitudes involves more complicated processes. The full meaning of measurement in the physical sciences is seen when that which is measured is an extensive quantity to which the addition theorem is applicable. Those traits of nature which are not subject to these conditions are not, strictly speaking, measurable. Briefly, the modern analysis of measurement calls attention to the following conditions: (1) we must be able to identify a standard character or state capable of indefinite repetition, (2) we must define some operation to determine when two magnitudes are equal, and (3) we must define some operation which will give meaning to the sum of two or more magnitudes. It may be urged that in the measurement of intensive magnitudes, the last of these conditions is absent. The fact, however, is that in the measurement of physical intensities such as temperature and the like, we always try to connect that which is measured with extensive elements such as distances on a thermometer scale, and this is very difficult to achieve in the social realm. Even if we limit ourselves to intensive social magnitudes such as pleasures or preferences, we find that statistics do not give us very much information, for our human preferences are proverbially inconsistent or highly variable in time according to incalculable subjective factors. We may put it in other terms by saying that in measuring human attitudes by questionnaires or records of preferences, we are dealing with the resultants of so many factors that the empirical results are seldom highly significant. For, as we saw before, where we do not isolate a single determinant we cannot expect to find a determinate relation. Somewhat similar warnings have been made in biology and in physics; and social phenomena are even more complicated because they include not only physical and biologic elements, but also such factors as fashion, linguistic attitudes and the like.

It becomes evident, then, that mere accumulation of social statistics will not enable us to isolate the relevant factors and to determine constant relations any more than we have been able to do with meteorologic statistics. Where we deal with fungible goods as we do in the realm of economics, we ignore all but the factor defined, such as price, amount of supply, etc. But how strong a desire for economic gain will outweigh tabus against forbidden food, working on the Sabbath, making graven images, or doing something which is dishonorable or results in loss of caste, we are hardly in a position to tell by statistical methods alone. Certainly the questionnaire method with children in the movies or students in the class room, selected because they can be readily induced to take the trouble to answer, can hardly claim to be adequate measurement. There is little evidence that the replies of other people will be the same as that of our selected group, and there is no way in which we can be assured that we have not fallen into the fallacy of selection no matter how much care we have exercised to choose at random. There are always characteristics of our group which we do not have in mind or reject as irrelevant but which may in fact be the most important factors in determining the results—for instance, our particular neighborhood, social class, temporary fashion or response to some special condition of the experiment which we have no thought of as significant. Thus, someone examines a number of school children in a given city and compares the standing of Jews and non-Jews. But the Jews happen to be of a special neighborhood where the parents follow certain occupations or all come from Turkey or Salonika, and are as different from Russian or German Jews as Turks are from Russians and Germans.

Another confusion in the attempt to use statistics in social measurement is the failure to discriminate between a phenomenon and people's opinion about it. Suppose you wish to measure that elusive quality, intellectual eminence. A leading psychologist who is entitled to our profound respect because of his many achievements, tries to dispose of the issue by asking a number of specialists to make an estimate and then treating their answers statistically. But is not this measuring rather a group of opinions? The belief that the average of a number of judgments by experts is necessarily more correct than the judgment of any one of them is based on the assumption that all these judgments are independent. But is that assumption always true? Experts in a given field read the same books or periodicals and are subject to vogues or fashions. When a vote is taken as to who is the leading psychologist, ablest baseball player, or most beautiful actress, the results may be more indicative of something about the voters for the time being than about that which is voted on.

The whole scheme of intelligence-testing assumes something whose nature is very ill-defined. Indeed, some of the leaders in this field first took the trouble to prove that there is no such thing as general intelligence and then proceeded to devise methods for measuring it. We must have clear ideas as to what it is that we are measuring.

There are other and subtler fallacies resulting from too great reliance on the technical procedures of statistical methods. Consider, for instance, some of the conclusions as to heredity by Galton and Karl Pearson. If we ignore the statistical methods and look at the matter critically, we can see that the extent of their material does not justify their conclusions. Surely a study of a thousand cases for two or three generations cannot determine the laws of inheritance, as to what traits are and what traits are not constant in environmental changes. I do not wish to deny that improved statistical methods enable us to guard against such errors. But it is elementary logic rather than technical statistics that enables us to realize this. I may in passing express the suspicion that biometric methods in genetics may, by emphasizing unit characters, be doing violence to the fact that in an organism various elements are not completely independent, and that statistical methods based on the assumption of such independence may lead us astray.

Bibliographic Note

A full bibliography of Statistical Inference and Probability up to 1927 will be found in the notes to Part V of Keynes, *Treatise on Probability*, and in the general bibliography which follows. Keynes omits Peirce's important essays on the Doctrine of Chances, the Probability of Induction and the Order of Nature, which appeared in *Popular Science Monthly*, March, April and June, 1878, and were reprinted in *Chance, Love and Logic* (edited by M. R. Cohen, pp. 61-130), and in his Collected Papers (edited by Weiss and Hartshorne). See also Mises, R. V., *Wahrscheinlichkeit Statistik Und Wahrheit*, 1928; and article on *Probability* in *Encyclopedia of Social Sciences*. See Reichenbach, H., *Wahrscheinlichkeitslehre*, especially pp. 119-120, 1935.

On the general statistical view of nature and the classical statistical mechanics, see Merz, *History of European Thought in the Nineteenth Century*, V. II, Ch. 7, 1904; and Josiah Royce, in *Science* for 1914. Also Frank, Ph., *Das Kausalgesetz und seine Grenzen*, 1930.

A full bibliography and comprehensive survey of the classical statistical mechanics of Maxwell, Boltzmann and Gibbs, see P. and T. Ehren-fest in *Encyklopädie der Mathematischen Wissenschaften*, Band IV, 2 ii.

For more recent statistical mechanics, see Hertz, in Vol. X of *Hand-buch der Physik*; Planck, *Eight Lectures on Theoretic Physics*, 1909; Tolman, R. C., *Statistical Mechanics*, 1927; Fowler, *Statistical Mechanics*, 1930; Dirac, *Quantum Mechanics*, 2d ed., 1935. The original memoirs of Schroedinger, De Broglie, Heisenberg, Jordan, Max Born, Sommerfeld, Bose and Einstein are clearly dealt with and referred to in Pauling and Wilson's *Introduction to Quantum Mechanics*, 1935.

VIII

Values, Norms and Science

1. *The Possibility of Normative Science*

The positivist theory of science conceives of facts as all on the same level, namely that of existence. But while it is true that as existents all facts are on the same level, human facts have the additional character, not shared by most physical facts, of being emotionally polarized, that is, the object of admiration or dislike, attraction or repulsion. This is what makes them causes of various levels of activity. We turn our faces away from anything repulsive, and we turn our faces towards objects of beauty or attraction. This active or directional character of human facts is somewhat like that which distinguishes the vector "seven miles north" from the scalar "seven miles," and is just as objective, as indeed are all facts of human conduct.

There is an old controversy between those who hold that facts of value are purely subjective, that is, identical with the mere fact that they are felt, and the view that there is some real difference, as a cause or ground for the distinction, between the valuable and the non-valuable. Now the fact that some things are liked and others are disliked is necessary but not sufficient for ethics—for, like any other science, ethics must be rational, that is, able to give reasons for such differences of attitude. When grounds of preference are made explicit, we call such formulations "norms" and the systematization and clarification of such norms is the basic subject matter of ethics.

The objection will at once be made that ethics is a science of what we ought to like and that is not a mere preference or a mere difference of attitude. This is perfectly correct as an objection to the theory that ethics is concerned only with preferences. But while preferences are a necessary element, without which human conduct is unintelligible, norms are more than preferences. Preferences are immediate and may be particular. Norms must be general, and in order to be rational must be consistent.

Moreover, to the extent that preference is a transitive relation, its objects can be arranged in series and thus form what the mathematician calls a field. A rational norm tells us which of two values we should prefer, because it assigns a reason or ground for such preference.

Norms are thus significant aspects of the human enterprise of living, knowing and understanding. Yet with the advent of modern science they have been relegated to a "second degree status of reality" in contradistinction to empirical fact.

Such has not always been the case in the course of intellectual history. The Greek classical conception included values and norms as proper objects of study and knowledge (ἐπιστήμη). The rejection of values as significant objects of study is part of the general modern reaction against the classical theory of deductive logic. The rapid rise of modern science, after the doctrine of final causes had been ejected as a ground of intelligibility, has led its more enthusiastic apologists to set up as a canon of intelligibility the "inductive method," a form of inquiry which is generally identified with empiricism, that is, a study of particular existential facts. The assertion of the antithetical nature of the inductive and deductive methods has been based upon a confusion as to the nature of scientific procedure. The elimination of judgments of value from scientific study is based upon this confusion.

The principal argument against the possibility of a normative science proceeds from the assumption that science can deal only with facts of existence to the conclusion that judgments of what ought to be are so arbitrary that no science of norms is possible.

This view of the nature of science is an exceedingly superficial one.

The notion that science deals only with the observation of facts originated during the Renaissance and was expressed most emphatically by Francis Bacon, who is still revered as the "father of scientific method" by those who pride themselves on following the inductive rather than the deductive method. Bacon's view rests on the assumption that the observation of facts is a simple process of mere recording. Actually, however, the determination of what the facts are is the end rather than the beginning of enquiry. Every enquirer must begin not with a *tabula rasa* for the recording of fresh facts, but with a fund of information. Discoveries in nature are not made by those who follow Bacon's precept and rid themselves of all anticipations of nature. The man who knows nothing about the subject may be free from all bias but he will not discover anything. The facts of nature do not stream into empty minds.

But while previous knowledge is necessary, it is not sufficient for the observation or discovery of new facts. We need ideas or hypotheses. It is only when we have an hypothesis that we have something to look for. Without ideas, nature is one big blooming confusion. The child begins, not with the observation of particulars, but with vague images. The child does not begin by seeing apple trees, chestnut trees, and others, and then generalizing. On the contrary, it takes considerable reflection and critical observation before the individual object is recognized for its specific qualities. Over two thousand years ago, Aristotle called our attention to the fact that an infant calls every man "father," and it certainly takes time before he distinguishes his father from other men.

Recognizing this intellectual element in perception, we can see that science is not a knowledge of mere particulars, but rather a knowledge of the way in which classes of things are related. Science views nature from the point of view of universal laws, and the progress of science consists in making such laws more certain, accurate, and systematically connected. This process is as applicable to the material of ethics as to the field of physics or mathematics. The fundamental fallacy of positivism is the assumption that facts of physical perception are in themselves definitely determinate and thus objective in a unique sense inapplicable to realms of value or pure mathematics. But, as James and others have shown, the facts of physical perception are definitely influenced by our interests.[1]

Scientific statements or propositions can be sharply distinguished from statements of history. The record of observations in a laboratory tells us merely what has happened. But a scientific law always takes the form of a universal proposition and asserts that a certain combination is impossible. Now the realm of the possible is applicable to the future as well as to the remote past. Hence, every observation, for purposes of science, is directed at a universal or repeatable aspect. But this repeatable aspect is abstract and the relations between such abstractions cannot be said to exist in the sense in which particulars exist. This has led positivists like Mach, Duhem, and Hans Vaihinger to assert that only particular sensations are real, and that all universals or mathematical entities are fictions. This view has at least the merit of recognizing that the common positivistic objections to ethical concepts are equally applicable to the concepts of physical science. But those who take this view have never been able to explain why it is that mathematical fictions have proved such a fruitful way of penetrating the secrets of nature, or why so many phenomena have been discovered by means of purely mathematical methods.

We can avoid these difficulties by rejecting the myth that nature consists simply of elements corresponding to sensations. In fact, the argument for this view is based upon the fallacy of reduction. A sentence is not composed of words alone, for if we take the words in a different order the sentence no longer remains the same. Similarly, while conscious life may be analyzed

[1] See the elaborate and convincing arguments of Professor Stuart in his essay, "Valuation as a Logical Process," in Dewey, *Studies in Logical Theory*, p. 227.

into elements called sensations, it is not true that sensations alone constitute our intellectual life. The order or relation between sensations is itself a part of the subject matter of psychology, as William James well recognized.

Thus the world of physics does not consist of isolated atoms or isolated qualities, and the world of ethics does not consist of isolated preferences. The world of physics, like the world of ethics, is a world in which there are real connections, and if we recognize the reality or objectivity of those connections, then we shall have no difficulty in recognizing that ideals are the proper subject matter not only of ethics and mathematics, but also of physical and other theoretic sciences. Thus, one of the first discoveries in mechanics, namely the law of the lever, formulates something which can never be actually realized. For the law of the lever assumes an absolutely rigid body without weight, but such absolutely rigid bodies do not exist in nature—certainly not in the world that we know. The laws of motion are formulated for ideal bodies whose masses can be concentrated into ideal points. The whole of thermodynamics is based upon considerations of what would happen in a frictionless engine, even though we know that such engines are impossible. Similarly, we talk of measuring an electric field by introducing an ideal point which would be repelled with a certain force without setting up an inductive current. These and numerous other examples indicate what is meant by saying that science is concerned with ideal entities and determines the character of existing objects by these ideal standards. Science, primarily, is not interested in any particular existing entity for its own sake. It is interested in building up ideal systems which are applicable to the existing world.

In view of the foregoing considerations, let us see in what sense the possibility of a normative science of social phenomena, or of ethics, or of law, can be upheld.

Discussion of the question whether the social studies can be properly called "scientific" appears to be, in the main, a quarrel about prestige and honor. It is evident that the degree of certainty and definiteness prevailing in mathematical physics cannot be attained in our knowledge of social phenomena, for the reason that social phenomena are much more complicated, and that the disinterestedness necessary for scientific pursuits is much more difficult of attainment in the social than in the physical realm. But if we should take the extreme position and say that the so-called social sciences are matters of mere opinion, the obvious reply is that some opinions are better founded than others; that an economic study which takes into account the actual supply of goods in certain markets, and the actual prices obtained for those goods, formulates certain relations which hold with a fair degree of approximation under prescribed conditions; and that such studies can well be called scientific in the sense that they employ the method of science.

We shall, therefore, use the term "social science" without prejudice and analyze the problem, to what extent the various social studies are in fact scientific.

Social sciences deal not only with what happens but with human desires and aspirations, and with human judgments as to whether various happenings are good or bad, useful or harmful, worthy of approval or disapproval. The exclusion of facts concerning aspirations and desires, as well as of normative judgments generally, from the body of knowledge which is called scientific, is the crux of a difficulty from which many centuries of controversy have emanated.

2. *The Classical Value Systems*

There are two historic attitudes on this point. The classical view can be traced to Plato and Aristotle. Just as there are fundamental principles which enable us to systematize our judgments of perception and thus give us a theory of nature, so we can attain to certain principles which enable us to organize our judgments of value, ethical or esthetic, into a rational system of judgments on human conduct. Against this view, there is the modern movement which is generally called positivism and which takes its cue from physical science (or what it supposes to

be the method of physical science), and urges that only questions
as to what actually happens can be the legitimate object of
scientific enquiry, and that study in the social field that aims
to be scientific must banish all concern with judgments of value,
since the latter are arbitrary and cannot be put under the causal
laws which are the essential trait of science. This controversy
has resulted in a voluminous literature which frequently emits
more heat than light.

The classical view may be seen at its best in Aristotle's ethics
and politics. In the field of ethics, the wise man will choose the
means that will bring about the harmony which we call happiness. Knowledge is thus the condition of virtue. It is well to note
that Aristotle's is essentially an aristocratic view. Not only is
knowledge necessary to attain the highest good, but one must
have the means to pursue the highest good, and those means are
health, wealth, and a well organized community. No one, therefore, can normally be expected to be virtuous unless he is so
well endowed. The virtuous are the children of good fortune.
Possibly the word "virtue" is misleading. The Greek word ἀρετή
might more accurately be translated as "excellence"—the object
of admiration.

Christian ethics replaced worldly excellence by the ideal of
holiness which made the highest good obtainable by those who
are poorly endowed by nature but who have the excellences of
spirit—faith, hope, and charity. The meek shall inherit the earth.
The most consistent philosophical expression of the latter view
is found in Kant's conception of ethics. Ethical science is concerned with all categorical duties. We are all under the obligation to obey the moral law, whether we like it or not. Indeed,
it seems as if there is more merit in obeying the law when we
do not like it, than in following the law out of natural inclination.

The Kantian ethics finds its most characteristic application in
the field of law. It is, according to Kant, the duty of the state
to punish criminals in exact proportion to the severity of the
crime. Thus if a society is to be disbanded, the last murderer

must be executed, else the blood of his victim will be on our heads.

There are two considerations in regard to the Kantian view which we must discriminate. First, there is the moral rigorism which is somewhat repulsive to the modern taste. The second point is the assumption of absolute necessity and uniformity of moral imperatives that are generally recognized although seldom followed. Thus Kant regards the duty to tell the truth as absolute; that is, subject to no exception or qualification. If a villain enters my house and wishes to kill my mother, I have no right to tell him a lie in order to save her life. This is the necessary consequence of what may be called the absolutistic conception of moral rules. Most people accept the principle, though they do not accept the result. The reason for this is that popular morality has from time immemorial been sanctioned by religion or propriety (the latter is in some cases even stronger and perhaps always more basic). We must not do certain things because they are not done. There is the terror of the unknown which surrounds any departure from the customary *mores*. Mankind, therefore, generally clings to the absolutistic conception of morality, even though only a few men are inclined to follow it consistently.

3. *The Challenge of Positivism in the Social Sciences*

Reflective thought, however, has not hesitated to challenge the absolutism of moral rules, since the Greek philosophers introduced the habit of free enquiry into human affairs. It has been observed that people's views as to what is right and wrong differ in different countries. Indeed, they differ for the same people at different times. Thus the marriage of a man with his sister on his father's, but not on his mother's, side, was considered perfectly proper in the time of Abraham or King David, but was regarded as incestuous in later times. This raises skepticism as to whether there is any inherent rightness or wrongness, whether it is not all a matter of arbitrary opinion. Just as the discovery of non-Euclidean geometry led to the bankruptcy of the old rationalism in geometry and physics, so the discovery of diversity of moral judgment led to the abandonment of the old rationalistic conception of morals or ethics. Riding on the wave of this relativism, positivistic philosophers like Lévy-Bruhl have tried to expound the nature of the social sciences without regard to any judgments of value. Their business as students of social phenomena is to describe what happens. The scientist must abandon his own prejudice or bias if his work is to be worthy of the name of science. We are familiar with this view in the field of history, economics, politics, jurisprudence, ethics, and linguistics. The empirical view which stresses the observation of facts as they actually occur can be seen clearly in the reaction against rationalistic history at the beginning of the nineteenth century. Similar to the reaction against the romantic *a priori Naturphilosophie* of Schelling, Hegel, and their followers, is the view best represented by Ranke, that the function of history and science is to get at the evidence and to describe things as they really happen. Actual history, however, shows that this is an inadequate ideal because it offers no ground for discriminating between important and unimportant facts.

The positivistic conception of scientific method when extended to history raises two issues. First, assuming that human events are subject to causal determinations, are judgments of importance or of approval or disapproval at all significant? Second, are judgments of importance or of approval or disapproval entirely arbitrary, or is there any way by which we can determine whether such judgments are well-founded or not?

As to the first point, it is clear that for the purpose of understanding history we must disabuse ourselves of our own personal moral standards, or even those of our contemporaries, if we wish to understand the past. Thus, it is a common error to suppose that the framers of the American Constitution were clear in their own minds as to whether they intended to give the courts power to declare statutes unconstitutional. This illustrates the point that we cannot always read into the past those issues that are clear and important to us. But while we must exercise this caution, we must not forget that issues of right and wrong form the substance of a large part of human history, and that we cannot understand what actually happened if we leave out of account what people felt about the right and wrong of the issues involved.

In regard to the second issue, the question may be put: Is it legitimate for the historian to consider alternative possibilities to the events which have happened? For instance, what was the objective in Alexander's mind when he invaded the Persian Empire? Surely it is relevant, if we wish to consider why he stopped to besiege the city of Tyre, to consider the general policy which made that act necessary. Might not Alexander have satisfied his world-conquering ambition if he had turned West instead of farther East? To say that the thing happened the way it did, is not at all illuminating. We can understand the significance of what did happen only if we contrast it with what might have happened. This measuring of alternatives is a simple matter in physics. It is, to be sure, a more difficult problem in human history. But it is not altogether devoid of evidence. We know, for instance, that without Alexander certain events would have been impossible, for in fact none of his generals could keep his empire together. So, likewise, do we know that without Napoleon the French generals could not conquer Northern Italy, for they actually failed to do so. The historian, therefore, must put himself imaginatively before the event in order to estimate the various possibilities of which the actual outcome is only one. For this purpose he must take into account the feelings and moral standards prevailing at the time of action. Unless we have reflected on the logic of moral judgments, we cannot understand why certain peoples in the past, or even in the present, have acted or are acting in ways which seem to us morally strange.

The historian must have a point of view in selecting his material: a point of view which determines what is important and what is unimportant in the confusing world of human events, and the category of importance is one of valuation. The safeguard against bias in writing history, as in the natural sciences, is not to indulge in useless resolutions to be free of bias, but rather to explore one's preconceptions, to make them explicit, and thus to multiply the number of hypotheses for the apprehension of historical significance.

The same aversion against normative judgments is evidenced in the field of jurisprudence. The historical school began as a reaction against the philosophy of natural rights, which had sought to revolutionize the world. Its dogma is that the concern of the jurist is to describe that which actually happens in legal development, and not to impose his own judgment. This, however, resulted in the conservative natural rights theory; that is, in a glorification of the *status quo* as desirable. Savigny, Maine and the late Mr. Carter are at one in distrusting deliberate changes of the law.

That positivism does not escape judgments of value, but only hides them, is most obvious in the writing of a leading French jurist, Duguit. Duguit starts out with the resolution that, as a scientist, he is not in any way interested in what ought to be, but is concerned merely to describe the law as it is. But what is the law? According to Duguit, it is a rule of conduct which promotes social solidarity. Suppose, however, that Parliament or our legislature enacts a rule which in effect makes for social disintegration. Many of our leading citizens think, rightly or wrongly, that this is actually what is happening today in Washington and elsewhere. Shall we say that such statutes are not law? M. Duguit has the courage of his confusion and says that it is up to the judges to decide whether a law is constitutional or not. But actually such decisions generally involve moral judgments of the individual judges, and M. Duguit himself condemns socialistic legislation as unpatriotic and thus immoral. Such a situation is not merely a matter of personal inconsistency. The fact is that all people who pretend to be indifferent to considerations of right and wrong actually make judgments of right and wrong, implicitly if not avowedly, and these judgments are not better by reason of their failure to receive explicit critical examination—just as judgments of metaphysics are not sounder because they are unavowed. In short, the fact is that we all do make judgments of value. As human beings we cannot avoid making such judgments. Is it not wisest to take the precaution to make these judgments as sound and as free of inconsistency as possible—as we do in all other fields of science?

The unsuccessful effort to avoid direct or explicit ethical judgments is also exemplified by American writers on jurisprudence who, under the influence of behavioristic psychology, urge that the science of law should have no other object than to study the course of actual decision. The law is what the judges decide. But what the judge in any case must look to as a guide to his decision is not a prediction of what he will do but rather a set of assumed principles of an ethical or normative nature.

The reaction against final causes dates back to the modern revival of the mechanistic view of nature. The explanation of physical and even biologic phenomena in terms of their purpose had proved sterile. For the purposes were those of the Author of nature, and His ways are past understanding. Nothing is thus determined and we have no way of finding out what is the true purpose, or the ways or means whereby the purposes are realized. That everything happens according to the will of Allah may be irrefutable, but it does not offer a path or way for scientific research. For this reason, Bacon referred to final causes as vestal virgins, chaste but unfruitful.

There can be no doubt that the method of looking for mechanisms which indicate how things come about has proved a most fruitful way of increasing human knowledge. And for this reason, writers on biologic and social science have thought that they could transform their studies into perfect sciences by following or adapting the causal, mechanical method of the sciences of physics and chemistry. But the discovery of precise mechanisms is a difficult matter in human realms and especially in social affairs. Our language has been framed for practical purposes rather than scientific purposes. It is, indeed, difficult to talk the language of mechanism or causation without making human purposes themselves causes. But how a purpose which is purely psychical can cause a change in the physical world, is a difficulty which has not been satisfactorily solved except for those who believe in magic. In any case, the causation of purpose is different from the type of connection which we call cause in physics.

In the biologic realm, the description of phenomena in terms of purpose is unavoidable so long as we do not know the precise mechanism. Thus we speak of the tendency of the organism to preserve itself, or the aim of nature to preserve the species, without believing that the aim is a real intention of conscious purpose. This manner of speech is merely analogical, *as if*.

It is well to note that the confusion which identifies the existential and the normative is not restricted to Aristotle and the Stoics. Most of us still regard "unnatural" or "artificial" as a term of disapproval, and we still speak of "unnatural" crimes as if they were due to causes beyond nature. Even scientists like Huxley speak of nature punishing people for breaking her laws, as if the law of property were a law of nature.

Psychoanalysis and the system of therapeutics based on it, assume a distinction between the healthy and the pathologic without inquiring as to what constitutes the difference between the two. When is a patient cured? If we answer, "When he is adjusted to his environment," we merely shift the issue to the question when a man is adjusted, and whether it may not be better for a man not to be adjusted to his environment or social milieu, whether he may not do better "to smash this sorry scheme of things entire."

We are thus constantly passing value judgments (in terms of final causes) when we speak of things as normal or abnormal, the average man, and especially when we use the term "pathologic." In biology, there is no difference between normal physiology and pathology, except in our point of view as to what we consider the end of the process. Those conditions which lead to death are generally called pathologic and yet there could be no life without catabolism, the breaking down of tissue. As Huxley put it, protoplasm manages to live by continually dying.

The behavioristic conception of ethics is exemplified in *The*

Ethics of Hercules by Professor Givler. A science of ethics, according to Professor Givler, must be mechanistic and deal with the human body. That is, it must be a branch of physiology, from which he draws the conclusion that the appropriate ethical ideal is Hercules rather than Cinderella. The man of brawn and physical achievement is the ideal rather than the dreamer of dreams. We may suppose that most Americans who have been indoctrinated with the gospel of efficiency, according to the system of Mr. Taylor, will agree with Givler's preference for the active as opposed to the contemplative life. But medieval as well as Hindu philosophers agree with Aristotle in evaluating the contemplative above the active life. In fact, it may be claimed that the energy of contemplation is more intense than that of muscular action. In any case Givler is appealing not to the science of physiology, with which he initiates his enquiry, but to an ethical judgment of preference. It is obvious that physiology cannot determine questions of ethics. The choice of a Herculean ideal is an individual preference which many may reject.

The attempt to dispense with all judgments of value in the field of economics had led to the so-called historical school of economics, which abandoned the search for economic laws and sought to understand economic life as historic phenomena. It is now generally agreed that while the historical school in economics has unearthed a great deal of interesting material for the economic sciences and has thus widened perspectives, it has failed to advance science precisely because of the fact that without a theory of human values it is powerless to discriminate between what is illuminating and what is not. In this connection, we can call attention to the writings of Thorstein Veblen who, though attempting to give us what seems a definitive refutation of the historical school as expounded by Schmoller, ultimately falls back upon very much the same thing in his conception of biological evolution as the norm for the economic pattern. But that which is the outcome of evolution is merely the existential, not always the most desirable. The last stage of any evolution may be that of degeneration, death and destruction.

Possibly one of the most illuminating illustrations of the inadequacy of the attempt to dispense with the notion of value in the social field is the science of linguistics. The old grammars laid down rules as to the correct form of diction. Good English is the English as spoken by the king, who, in point of historic fact, was generally either a Frenchman, a Welshman, a Scot, or a German. The positivistic reaction is to view language as a natural phenomenon so that the science of language is a physical science. This has tended to make our linguistics a branch of phonology. Recently, however, students of linguistics have begun to realize that language is an instrument for human purposes, and that the question of the extent to which it serves these purposes is an indispensable part of any adequate science.

4. Integrating Value Judgments

The foregoing considerations show the limitations of the positivistic approach to the question of value judgments in the social field. On strictly logical grounds the fallacy is the same as the fallacy of those who believe that science can be built up by pure induction. The essence of the fallacy is the assumption that the facts constitute the starting point of inquiry, whereas they are the ends to be achieved by inquiry. The progress of science consists in formulating hypotheses based upon the best available knowledge and anticipating new situations which can be experimentally brought into being so that greater determination can be achieved. From this point of view, ethical systems can be made scientific by developing adequate hypotheses as to what is good or bad, or what is necessary in order to achieve certain ends. All agree that pure mathematics is a science, yet it can readily be put into the normative form. Thus to have a perfect square we must add certain quantities. In order that a series should have a limit it must have certain characteristics, etc. And so in order to attain a certain harmony of our human purposes certain cautions must be observed. This kind of problem involves two elements. First, it involves the element of causation.

If I do certain things, certain consequences will follow. Such judgments must obviously be based on knowledge of the actual effects of the acts in question. But, as has been indicated earlier, the mere knowledge that certain things will follow is not sufficient to determine whether they are desirable or not.

One of the obvious facts of human nature is that our unhappiness comes not only from the fact that we cannot have what we want, but very often we are most miserable because we succeed in getting what we thought we wanted. Wisdom, therefore, consists in surveying our various conflicting desires with a view to the attainment of a harmony, or a maximum of happiness. A man may prefer a short but a merry life. Another may prefer suicide. But, if we regard our life as a continuing one, that is, if we have some regard for our own personality, we must integrate all of our desires into one coherent system, so that we can attain self-respect. Just as all of our judgments of perception of nature can be integrated by physical science into a view of the world, so may our judgments of preference be integrated with them into a view of the most desirable mode of life.

Ethical issues arise when, in fact, I ask which of a number of possibilities I should choose or approve.

We must at all times draw a distinction between existence and value; between considerations *de facto* and *de jure*. That I do like certain things, is an assertion of fact; that I ought to like certain things, or that somebody is evil-minded in that he likes the wrong things, is a moral assertion. Not everything that exists has a right to exist. It is quite obvious that the fact that I have liked certain things is not the complete justification for continuing to like them, or a sufficient reason why someone else should like them. If we believe in the growth of wisdom or education, then tastes are worth cultivating. This, of course, does not mean that we can always make a man like what he does not like. It does mean, however, that we realize by reflection that some of our habits produce results which we do not like or approve. That is to say, reflection makes clear to us the causes of conflict within our lives. And this consciousness or recognition of a conflict helps us to some extent in overcoming it, and thus brings about a better or happier state of mind and life. A theory of desires will give us the raw materials of ethics, not a complete account of it. A normative science of ethics may aim at a final synthesis which will co-ordinate all of our various desires and harmonize them, so that our lives will be free from the tortures which the absence of self-knowledge creates.

5. *The Difficulties of Ethical Science*

The motive behind a good deal of the positivistic effort to free social science of all ethical judgments is the combination of a praiseworthy desire to attain scientific understanding of social problems and a feeling that since ethics cannot possibly be scientific, social studies can achieve the status of science only by rigorously ridding themselves of all ethical elements. But the failure of all efforts to rid social studies of ethical elements should lead to a re-examination of the original positivistic assumption that scientific methods cannot be applied to judgments of what ought to be. We have seen that many of the imagined obstacles to scientific treatment of ethical problems are wholly fictitious. Such a fictitious obstacle, for example, is the view that science can deal only with what actually exists. Yet beyond such fictitious obstacles to scientific method in the field of ethics there are certain very substantial difficulties which help to account for the low intellectual level of most ethical discussion.

Perhaps the most important difficulty in the attainment of scientific standards in ethical judgments is the tendency to view incomplete expressions, which are neither true nor false, as if they were propositions—complete, definite, and necessarily either true or false. The tendency to assume that we have achieved complete definiteness when we are really very far from attaining any such goal, is not, of course, restricted to the field of ethical judgments. It exists in all domains of human discourse—even among logicians, who are currently prone to assume that we can create propositions in the manner of the Lord by uttering the words,

"Let p be a proposition." Elsewhere we have spoken of the humanly inevitable incompleteness of the meanings that are attached to all symbols,[2] and of the "twilight zones" that are the logical consequence of this incompleteness,[3] but the erroneous assumption of completeness and definiteness is particularly prevalent and particularly serious in the field of ethics.

Four factors contribute to this result:

In the first place, the field of ethics is one of manifold complexity, in which there is more room for unnoticed gaps and ambiguities in discourse than is the case with simpler fields like geometry or chemistry.

In the second place, ethical propositions are so often regarded as self-evident that we seldom think of questioning their definiteness.

In the third place, the needs of pedagogy impose upon religious and other moral teachers of the immature the practical need of simplifying precepts by omitting qualifications and refinements. This practical need frequently takes the perverted form of opposing as "casuistical" all efforts at a scientific refining of the raw materials of ethical opinion.

Finally, there is the fact that while we do not have to decide at a moment's notice whether the earth is to rotate around its axis at a slowly decreasing velocity, we do have to make practical judgments in the field of ethics before there is time to weigh all relevant considerations and qualifications. This practical need for making decisions in the absence of all the facts one may recognize without making it the basis for a perverted condemnation of scientific effort in ethical fields.

The ideal of definiteness in ethical judgment remains a valid scientific ideal even though it be incapable of complete human attainment. We can only hope that those obstacles to the attainment of this ideal which are inherent in the complexity of the subject will yield to the same sort of patient analysis that has been productive of clarity in other scientific fields. More serious

[2] See *supra*, p. 30 ff.
[3] See *supra*, p. 67 ff.

are those obstacles that arise from our own attitudes to ethical inquiry. A wise man has said that the reason we do not more often attain the truth in social fields is that we do not want to. Such subjective obstacles we can overcome only if we are able to place the search for truth above a concern with the immediate moral consequences of our analysis. Just as the great advances of modern physical science have been made by men whose passion for understanding the facts of nature was greater than any concern with the practical social effects likely to follow from their inquiries, so the great advances of the future in ethical understanding are likely to be achieved only by those who are firmly resolved to press ethical inquiry to its logical limit without regard to immediate practical consequences.

Questioning basic moral assumptions is undoubtedly a dangerous business that may well lead immediately to an undermining of accepted moral standards. But how can more adequate moral standards be formulated if every variation from accepted traditional norms is condemned in advance? To have questioned one's own most cherished ideals, as Justice Holmes has said, is the mark of a civilized man. Such questioning may result in the reaffirmation of one's ethical assumptions, fortified by the elimination of spurious attacks, or it may result in the rejection of views that cannot be consistently maintained; but in almost all cases it results in a refinement of the issues and concepts with which we started and thus in a more civilized appreciation of the manifold needs and potentialities of the human spirit.

This process of clarification and refinement may, to be sure, produce formulas overly complex for the business of everyday life, but the approximations that we make after detailed analysis of a problem are more likely to be adequate than those we accepted prior to such analysis. We may recognize that a given law will produce social harm in one case out of every hundred in which it is applied, and yet recognize at the same time that the law is a valid, practical approximation because the social cost of further qualifying the law to remove that case from its purview would be more serious than the particular injury which might thereby be avoided. So we may decide that at certain levels of moral pedagogy, or on occasions when prompt practical decisions will have to be made, we shall have to deal in rough generalizations just as we use rough approximations for the value of π or the square root of two in teaching engineering or in making rapid calculations. But these practical concessions to human needs and human limitations should not obstruct the paths to greater accuracy that science offers, and in other circumstances practical needs may demand this greater accuracy. No slogan is more productive of obscurantism than the cliché "true in theory, but wrong in practice." What is wrong in practice must be wrong in theory unless the theory itself is wrong. And if our theory is wrong it is certainly more intelligent to try to set it right by making appropriate qualifications than to attempt blindly to cling both to the theory and to the fact that contradicts it on the pretext that theories and facts belong to different worlds. In the long run, only those moral theories that are rigorously examined and continually refined are able to withstand the shifting winds of fashion and circumstance. But even if this were not the case, and even if the process of questioning ethical assumptions were as productive of anarchy and confusion as the narrowest of obscurantists has ever contended, it would still be true that only through this process of questioning can the ideal of a scientific treatment of ethical problems be approached.

6. Clarifying Ethical Judgments

Let us then look more closely at the various types of incompleteness that appear in ethical discourse. Four principal sources of such incompleteness may conveniently be distinguished.

1. *Functional Criticism.* When we speak of a good lawyer or a bad soldier we commonly mean to assert that a human being does or does not efficiently perform the function of a social role in which he has been cast. In the same sense we may speak of a good phonograph or a poor camera or a medicine good for

dysentery. But applying such adjectives does not preclude us from asking whether lawyers or soldiers ought to carry out their traditional tasks efficiently or inefficiently, or whether the traditional norms in question should be revised. Only confusion results from mistaking an efficiency rating for a moral judgment. If our characterization of a particular lawyer or soldier in terms of his accepted function is intended to be only an efficiency rating we can profitably dispense with moral categories in such judgment. If, on the other hand, we intend to pass a moral judgment upon a soldier or lawyer we must recognize that any such judgment is incomplete unless it involves a consideration of the entire field of values to which the individual's existence is relevant. Indeed it is precisely this all-inclusiveness that distinguishes moral criticism from all other forms of criticism.

2. *Instrumental and Intrinsic Value.* It is ancient wisdom that while the value of many things results from their consequences certain things have value regardless of consequences. Otherwise the pursuit of values would be an infinite regress. If love, the search for truth, and the contemplation of beauty are goods in their own right, needing no justification in terms of their consequences, the same can hardly be said of many other things to which we commonly apply ethical categories. The "oughts" of everyday life are commonly predicated upon the connection between certain types of conduct and the consequences of such conduct for ourselves and for others. While the assumption of such causal connections is not in itself an ethical matter, most ethical judgments incorporate just such factual assumptions. So long as such assumptions remain unavowed they are likely to be the source of interminable misunderstandings and fruitless controversies. The disagreements of those who defend and oppose nationalism, for example, may represent ultimate differences of valuation or they may represent different opinions as to the factual consequences of nationalism. In the latter case scientific analysis of a non-ethical character may suffice to bring a decision; in the former case, such a procedure would be fruitless.

We can approach this matter in another way by saying that

the application of ethical concepts like good, better, or ought to any subject of discourse cannot be definite unless the subject is definite. And part of any subject of ethical judgment is its capacity to produce effects on human lives. Only as we approach clarity and definiteness in our conception of the causal efficacy of that which we are judging can we approach clarity and definiteness in our ethical judgments.

3. *The Objects of Ethical Judgment.* The confusions that arise from inadequate knowledge of the effects of acts and events upon which we pass moral judgment are similar to the confusions that arise from other forms of inadequacy in defining the objects of value judgments. People commonly speak of stealing, for example, as a perfectly definite concept, from which it follows that the commandment "Thou shalt not steal" has a single and perfectly definite meaning. But a moment's reflection shows that stealing involves the concept of "another person's property" and what is the whole of the civil law of property, with its indefinite multitude of ramifications of title and contract, if it is not an attempt to give added definiteness to this idea? Shall we say that one who utters the commandment "Thou shalt not steal" has in mind a complete set of criteria to determine whether or not any given act amounts to stealing? Is it not more realistic to regard the assertion "stealing is wrong" as an incomplete symbol, as something which points to a systematic scientific development in which the incompleteness of the symbol may be reduced? From this standpoint ethical certainty is not a brute datum with which the unreflective conscience starts but rather a rational ideal which we can approach only through a process of refinement and qualification.

Typically those who, like Kant, maintain the absolute truth of such propositions as "Lying is wrong" are called absolutists, and those who insist that such propositions need qualification in terms of circumstances are thought of as relativists. Relativism in this sense is thought of as the enemy of ethical certainty. This, I submit, is a perversion of the truth. Once we recognize the incompleteness of our everyday ethical judgments, in which the vague concepts of common discourse create twilight zones that mock all simple moral bifurcations, we can see that there is no certainty in the indefinitenesses and incompletenesses of common moral dogmas. To the extent that qualification is necessary to attain definiteness it is a condition of sound ethics. If this be called relativism, then relativism is essential to ethics as it is to any other field of thought that operates with the clumsy instruments of everyday discourse.

4. *The Relativity of Ethical Standards.* It may well be that even if we attained complete definiteness and certainty with respect to the object of an ethical judgment, there would still remain an uneliminable variability in the ethical standard to be applied to such object. Certainly logic does not provide us with a means for unifying all the various ethical standards which men have invoked or of proving the ultimate truth of any one standard. It may well be that two individuals, applying divergent but equally valid standards, can say of the same act, "This ought to be done" and "This ought not to be done," without contradicting each other, just as two people facing each other across a table can say of the same objects on a table, "Object A is to the right of B" and "Object A is to the left of B." If this ultimate ethical relativism be justified, then no ethical judgment can be complete or perfectly definite unless the standard involved in the judgment is precisely identified. To appraise the arguments that have been made for and against ethical relativism is not within the scope of this study. What is pertinent is the recognition that in ethical judgments the sources of indefiniteness may lie in the ethical predicate as well as in the factual subject, and this is something that even ethical absolutists may well admit. Certainly, as Bentham pointed out, people do use all the terms of the ethical armory in many different ways, and only by disengaging precise meanings from the ambiguity of incomplete symbols can we approach the definiteness which will permit us to apply to ethical discourse the logical standards that apply to genuine propositions.

This process of clarification may or may not reveal a basic and ultimate uniformity in human ethical perceptions. But at least it can free us from the twin evils of the vicious absolutism that, by ignoring the variability of human tastes and objectives, would condemn all mankind to a Procrustean bed and, on the other hand, the vicious relativism that, by denying all universal principles and objective truths, would imprison each of us in an isolated subjective world. Logic is concerned with a common world. Its processes may help us to locate such a world within the apparent chaos and discord of conflicting human ideals.

Meanwhile let us not forget that whatever high purposes a clarification of ethical discourse may serve in human civilization, the pursuit of ethical truth, like other high adventures of the human spirit, is itself a good.

IX

Logic and the World Order

1. *The Presuppositions of Logic*

The kind of world which logic assumes is that of propositions denoting states of affairs which are connected by threads of identity, so that we have unity in diversity. If A implies B, A and B cannot be altogether disparate or unconnected. But if they were completely or numerically identical without any difference we could not distinguish between A and B. This conception of unity in diversity will enable us to get rid of certain widespread fallacies.

The earliest of these fallacies and the most radical of them all is the argument that all propositions are either tautologies or else false, since to say that *John is honest,* or that *Smith is white,* is, if not a tautology, absurd,—for how can white be identical with Smith? The monists generally have built up a whole system of metaphysics upon this difficulty: a difficulty, however, which vanishes if we realize that every proposition, at least of the subject-attribute type, asserts an element of identity between different things, and that the identity has no meaning apart from difference, just as two things cannot be different unless they are, in some respects, objects of some one class—at least both are objects of consideration in the same context.

The converse of this fallacy is to assume that if two things are different they cannot also be identical in some respects. This takes the form of false alternatives. If poverty and ignorance are not identical, which is the cause of which? If religious and economic motives are not identical, which is primary and which is the *derivative?* Is our opponent a knave or a fool? Did the Roman Republic decline because of moral, economic, or biologic factors? Any attempt to disprove one of these possibilities by establishing one of the others assumes that these factors are mutually exclusive. But that assumption is seldom true outside of rigorous mathematical considerations.

Logic cannot be confined to the world of existence—meaning by the latter, actual existence—for science is concerned with the weighing of evidence and that means with the weighing of rival hypotheses. We must, therefore, be able to deduce the consequences of false propositions, that is, of propositions which assert either the non-existence of what does exist, or the existence of what does not exist.

However, it is necessary to be on guard against the tendency to conceive the world of possibility as a mere ghost of the actual, having no position in time or space. We must distinguish between bare possibility and the possibilities of any existing object. Bare or abstract possibility is a term by which we designate the class of possible objects or transformations. Concrete possibilities, however, are functions of existing objects, and if there were no world at all there would be no possibility in that sense. Concretely, we cannot describe any physical object, say a particle of iron, except in terms of the processes to which it can be subjected, that is, its possibilities. In this sense the possibilities constitute what we call the nature of the object, that is, its character or its essence, not its existence. Thus, any proof of the existence of an object must take us beyond logic and must include the assumption of some empirical observation which contains a non-logical element. If we assume Euclid's axioms it can be shown that the sum of the angles of a triangle must necessarily be equal to two right angles. But we cannot prove that there are any triangles in this world, and the assertion that a given drawing or object is triangular cannot be deduced from any wider propositions except if we make the empirical judgment that it has certain properties which we have agreed to call triangular. The fact, however, that it has those properties cannot be deduced. It is impossible to deduce particular material propositions from general principles.

Moreover, logic presupposes a world in which there is some systematic connection between things. But deduction or reasoning does not proceed from the totality of all things (as Spinoza seems to have reasoned) but rather from some formulated proposition to some other which it implies. This brings us to a paradox. If it be true that there is nothing in the conclusion which is not contained in the premises, of what possible value can logic be in the progress of science? The paradox disappears if we look at the actual facts of mathematics and realize how many new propositions in that field are discovered almost every day. And yet every one of these new propositions can be logically or rigorously demonstrated. The answer, of course, is that we must distinguish between *novelty,* the psychologic factor, and the logical connection between premises and conclusions. It is a crude metaphor to assert that the conclusion is contamed in the premises—as if the premises were a box and the conclusions were the objects in it. Conclusions are necessitated by the premises because if we follow certain rules of logic all alternative conclusions are shown to be impossible. By ruling out certain combinations of premises and conclusions we achieve determinate results. In this development of limited possibilities lies the fruitfulness of logic. Mathematics is thus productive as well as deductive. It is an exploration of the field of possibility just as truly as astronomy is an exploration of the field of stellar motions.

This connection of logic with theoretic science should warn us against the popular fallacy that a proposition may be true theoretically but not practically. Those who thus reject theory sometimes possess a sound perception but a highly inaccurate one. That which is true cannot be false, and if anything is true theoretically it is foolish to regard it as in any sense false. But, of course, a theory even if true may be inadequate. Indeed, generally speaking, no theory can exhaust all that is involved in the existence of any object however limited. If *per impossibile* any theory were as complicated as the actual facts, it would have no real value. All theory is a simplification and therefore incomplete. However, to despise theory is the essence of unwisdom, and those who quote Goethe as the authority for the statement, "gray is all theory," forget that this is the advice of Mephistopheles to corrupt the callow student.

Logic thus does not provide the food which sustains our intellectual life. That must come from our factual knowledge and insight. Logic also may be denied the characterization of being the motive power which sets inquiry going. It is, however, like the hydrochloric acid in our stomach that helps to digest our food. It is the antiseptic of our intellectual life which prevents our food from poisoning us. For the impressions we take into our minds will confuse us unless we order them according to some logical principle.

As form implies matter, logic implies something which is more than form. This may be referred to as the principle of polarity, and we can see its application in the most developed of our sciences, such as mathematical physics. It is impossible to have laws except of phenomena which are not themselves merely laws or universals. There is a contingent element in the very existence of the specific laws which formulate the nature of phenomena.

The association of logic with knowledge or the theory of knowledge has been used by writers like Green and other idealists to prove an idealistic view of the world—as if knowledge could create the object known. This, of course, is the Kantian argument that the mind unites the elements of sensation into coherent objects by means of its own categories or rules of synthesis. Now it would take us far afield to discuss the truth of the Kantian deduction of the categories. What is relevant, however, is to note the admission on the part of Kant's followers, from Schelling to Green, that it is not the individual mind of you or me that makes the synthesis of the world, though each one of us may help by his study and reflection to clarify his own views.

The mind that builds the world or creates it, is a mind that also creates our ancestors. If we substitute "God" or "the world process" for the word "mind" we shall not in any way change the nature of the argument. What Kant's transcendental argument, therefore, proves is that before we discover order in the world, the order must already be there and this is sufficient for all practical purposes of science or action.

Moreover, logic cannot prove that the world has any special material character, or that it is designed for a special purpose. All proofs, therefore, of the existence of God, of the immortality of the soul, or of the obligation to tell the truth at all times require as a premise some material assumption in the sense of some proposition which has material content, just as no proposition of physics can be proved from pure logic. But by the same token, there can be no disproof of any metaphysical or ethical proposition by logic alone.

There have, however, been recent attempts to rule out metaphysical and ethical issues on the ground that they are essentially meaningless. And this has been achieved by defining meaning in terms of physical operations. This, however, obviously begs the question. What it really does, in other words, is to assume a materialistic metaphysics in the sense that it assumes that no other entities are possible. We may not wish to quarrel with the truth of this proposition as a conclusion, but it is obviously an assumption which has a legitimate alternative, to wit: that there are more things in heaven and earth than are dreamed of by the materialists, even assuming that their dreams are material. The materialist may say that the assertion of other possibilities is meaningless to him. That is probably true, but it is not the same thing as saying it is necessarily meaningless to everyone else. The question, for instance, whether the world is run according to some quasi-human plan or not, whether we have within us something more than temporal consciousness, something which death will not completely destroy, so that some kind of self-identity will remain after death—these are questions for which the evidence may be insufficient or even preponderantly negative. No one, it seems to me, has a right to say that these questions, which have interested mankind more than have the questions of physical science, are inherently meaningless—though obviously they have no meaning for those who prefer not to see their meaning. None are so blind as those who do not wish to see.

2. *The Role of Logic in Human Affairs*

What is the function of logic in human affairs? We may properly appreciate the import of this question if we reflect upon the great mass of protest or indignation against "logic chopping." It must be confessed that while among the world's great heroes the religious teachers, the moralists, the poets, the artists, are regarded as saviors of mankind, few, if any, of the logicians have been placed among the foremost rank. The Renaissance and the various forms of Romanticism since then have never tired of denouncing the inhuman futility of scholastic pedantry, witness Erasmus, Luther and Bacon. We can, of course, explain this by the undoubted fact that science never has been or can be popular. Close reasoning is an arduous undertaking for which few have the opportunity, the equipment and the inclination. Moreover, the will to illusion is a powerful and all-pervasive factor. Unless we realize the pleasant character of illusion, as similar to that of intoxicating liquors, fumes, or physical gyrations, we cannot understand the course of human history. Nevertheless, when all is said, there is still a core of sound sense in the distrust of logic. But as in all other instances, common sense, even when sound, is seldom accurate. The objection to logic is really directed against its abuse, just as the objection to dangerous knives is not that they cut, but that foolish or unskillful people cut the wrong objects. Under the pretense of being logical, people have proved the wrong things by assuming false premises. This has been notably the case in the law. So-called strong judges give inhuman decisions not because they are logical but because they dogmatically refuse to analyze adequately their premises, refusing to invoke humane analogies with which every legal system is replete.

Those who by logic prove the worse to be the better cause, do so by some trick which logic itself can detect. The cure for the misuse of logic is the sound employment of logic. But while logic is a necessary condition for the attainment of the truth, it is not sufficient in itself. That which we prove depends upon premises or previous knowledge, and logic alone cannot supply us with material information. It must be admitted that just as the devil can quote the Scriptures, so may charlatans and impostors use good logic to pervert the truth and to spread error. To guard against this, we need factual knowledge as well as sound logic.

The answer to the question, "What is the function of logic?" can be put in another way. Logic insofar as it is a science has as its aim, like any other science, the promotion of right understanding. All other purposes must necessarily be subordinated.

There are, of course, those who take it for granted that pure science exists only for its practical applications. But a logician may well ask, "What is a practical application?" If we take "practical" in its narrowest sense, as that which has to do with what men pursue in their daily affairs, this doctrine would be equivalent to the assertion that the end of life is to engage in buying and selling, in producing goods, etc., and that thought is valuable only insofar as it helps in these activities. This view is sometimes supported by the biologic argument that since thought is a product of evolution it must have survival value. The latter contention, however, is quite gratuitous. Not everything that is the product of evolution has survival value. If that were the case, we could not explain why certain species have disappeared in the course of nature's history. There are pathogenic developments for which no possible survival value can be discovered. Moreover, if we take intelligence, as such, there is no evidence that it promotes an excess of births over deaths, which is the basis of biologic survival. Indeed, there is no evidence to oppose the view that intelligence as applied, for instance, to war may result in the elimination of the human race from the terrestrial area. This is not to deny that a certain amount of intelligence will help people in their business, nor can one deny that it is a good thing that this should be the case. Whatever aid logic can bring to us in dealing with the problems of human life, should be welcome. What can be insisted upon is that we must not make these practical aims all-inclusive or exclusive of the purely theoretic interest.

Man's theoretic interest has a natural origin in what is called curiosity. Wonder about the world need not be concerned about practical applications. We can be and are, in fact, interested in many things which we will never be able to apply in what is ordinarily called practical life. Gossip, for instance, is not actuated by any strict practical motive. We wish to know what certain people are doing for a reason similar to that which makes us want to whistle or to dance. The exercise of our brain-power is, under certain conditions, just as delightful as the exercise of any other power.

To the foregoing, the moralist may object that this views logic as a game, and that games are not part of the serious business of living. This, however, is a very questionable doctrine even from an ethical point of view. It would certainly be absurd to suppose that the appreciation of art should justify itself by practical applications. If the vision of beauty is its own excuse for being, why should not the vision of truth be so regarded. Indeed, is it not true that all useful things acquire their value because they minister to things which are not useful, but are ends in themselves? Utility is not the end of life but a means to good living, of which the exercise of our diverse energies is the substance.

We may, however, put this in a different light by saying that the exercise of thought along logical lines is the great liberation, or, at any rate, the basis of all civilization. We are all creatures of circumstance; we are all born in certain social groups and we acquire the beliefs as well as the customs of that group. Those ideas to which we are accustomed seem to us self-evident when our first reaction against those who do not share our beliefs is to regard them as inferiors or perverts. The only way to overcome this initial dogmatism which is the basis of all fanaticism is by formulating our position in logical form so that we can see that we have taken certain things for granted, and that someone may from a purely logical point of view start with the denial of what we have asserted. Of course, this does not apply to the principles of logic themselves, but it does apply to all material propositions. Every material proposition has an intelligible alternative if our proposition can be accurately expressed. Logic thus becomes an instrument for showing us the number of hypotheses other than those which we have taken for granted. The way to make progress in any field of learning is not by resolving to free ourselves of dogmatic assumptions—such resolutions are vain—but by making clear to ourselves what are the various assumptions that are possible, and thus envisaging our position as one of a great number. This widens our sympathetic understanding and breaks the backbone of fanaticism. It makes us humble because it indicates to us that ultimately we cannot prove the truth of our fundamental assumptions, for our fundamental assumptions determine the kind of a world which we can perceive and the world of phenomena is wider than that of our knowledge.

Logic teaches us, therefore, not to undertake vain proofs; it teaches us not to attempt to disprove the beliefs of those who really differ from us in fundamental principles. We can successfully argue only with those who start from the same premises as we do. If our opponent starts from entirely different premises then there can be no question of conclusive proof, although we may be able to induce our neighbor to question his fundamental assumptions by pointing out to him the dubious character of the consequences which follow from his assumed principles. Tolerance, the avoidance of fanaticism, and above all a wider and clearer view of the nature of our beliefs and their necessary consequences, is thus a goal or end which the development of logic serves. In this sense logic is a necessary element of any liberal civilization.

APPENDIX

TWO MASTERS OF LOGIC

1. F. H. Bradley

2. John Dewey

1

F. H. Bradley [1]

The first edition of Bradley's *Principles of Logic* appeared more than forty years ago. It was at once recognized as epoch-making; and it has since remained a classic in a domain which has shown more definite progress than any other field of philosophy. Though his writings are always models of clear and masterful English—his diction and sentences have the noble terseness of poetry—the inherent difficulty of his abstruse and close-knitted thought has made Mr. Bradley practically unknown to the public at large. The latest edition of the Britannica does not notice him, though it has a short article on his clerical half-brother. Yet for three decades before his recent death he had been placed by the consensus of the competent among the greatest figures in the history of philosophy, the subtlest and most incisive thinker that the English-speaking world has produced since Hume; and slow-moving England finally added to the lasting prestige of its great Order of Merit by joining his name to those of Thomas Hardy and others. Characteristically enough, though no important English-speaking philosopher in the last forty years has been uninfluenced by him, there is hardly a single one today who professes to be his disciple.

Let us recall the intellectual situation, when this book arrived on the scene in the eighties of the last century. The complacent orthodoxy which had bound the English mind since the French

[1] This review of *The Principles of Logic,* by F. H. Bradley, was published in *The New Republic,* vol. 50 (1927), p. 164.

Revolution, had been shaken to its roots by the historical or "higher" criticism of the Bible, and by the scientific movement represented by such names as Darwin, Lyle and Huxley. Those who clung to the human values which the prevailing Christianity served to enshrine, felt that the triumph of the new materialistic tendencies meant the degradation of man and the death of all that had been held noble and spiritual. Yet how was the relentless accumulation of facts by the enemy to be met? Out of this dilemma was born the new idealistic movement led by T. H. Green, the brothers Caird, and others. By the use of German philosophy it found a way of accepting the main "results" of science, such as the theory of evolution, while rejecting the short-sighted emphasis on matter and sensations which characterized the positivistic school. It kept the historic forms of Protestant Christianity by giving them a new liberalized interpretation, seemingly in harmony with science and historical scholarship. It was this synthetic phase of the new idealism which aroused most enthusiasm and attracted men like Josiah Royce and the youthful John Dewey in this country.

The appearance of this work of Bradley's on logic in 1883 was generally viewed as a great triumph for the idealistic school. It revealed a great thinker who could see far deeper than the surface-clarity of Mill, and could with his dialectic rapier cut to shreds the loose, if not shabby, patch-work which passed as the English philosophy of experience. Just as Mill's *Examination of Hamilton* had proved a death blow to the previously prevailing union of Scotch "common sense" and dilute transcendentalism, so Bradley's *Logic* definitely overthrew the intellectual prestige of Mill's empiricistic logic. Empiricism itself, of course, has too much vitality and too many roots in human thought to be ever completely eliminated. But it never recovered from the blows dealt in this book. Its life since then has been largely subterranean and on the defensive. When it ventures forth aggressively into the open, as in some of the writings of William James, it shows a painful consciousness and the outer marks of the blows which it had thus received. In the end, also, despite his protests, James's idea of pure experience is less like that of Mill and more like Bradley's Absolute in which clear concepts and logical relations are swallowed up in an ineffable Reality.

Bradley's *Logic,* however, was too powerful and too disinterested to stop with the damage it inflicted on the old unimaginative empiricism. It carried its dialectic forward to a point where it also undermined the dogmatism of the new idealism. In behalf of our so-called higher interests, the philosophy of Kant and Hegel had tried to show that any effort to regard the objects of common sense and material science as ultimate reality, must involve self-contradiction. Taking up this cue Bradley pursued it with relentless thoroughness. Very little of the ideology and intellectual structure of the new idealism itself escaped the marvelously double-edged sword of his powerful logic. No wonder that philosophers generally preferred to make smart demonstrations against him rather than come to close grips with him. It is, of course, relatively easy to reject his whole method on the ground that it is too skeptical and leaves us with no comforting certainties. It is tempting to sum up his philosophy with the statement: The world of reality is rational and everything in it is a necessary contradiction. But the fatal weakness of the neo-Hegelian idealistic doctrines based on such concepts as *the self, the good,* etc., had been revealed once for all, and even their brave defense by Josiah Royce could not save them. A new generation of men like G. E. Moore and Bertrand Russell, trained in Bradley's logic though not sharing his positive premises, swept through the pretended logical proofs of the new idealism and left it as a memory of fine piety rather than of high intellectual achievement.

Thus it came to pass that a life-long invalid, separated almost entirely from the march of the world's affairs, and even from the progress of science, has yet managed to mold the course of philosophic thought and affect powerfully the methods and standards of its argumentation. Bradley was able to do this primarily because he added to his penetrating logic a rare courage in the pursuit of truth to the bitter end. We may perhaps put it more adequately by saying that Bradley stands head and shoulders above the multitude of clever advocates or passionate propagandists for good causes, by his high sensitiveness to the essential tragedy of human thought itself—its unavoidable task and its inescapable frustration. Long before James, Bergson, and lesser men began to harp on the immediate sense of "life" that escapes the mechanical net of "logic," Bradley wrote in the first edition of this book the matchlessly eloquent protest against the view that the world of our joys and sufferings is naught but a "ballet of bloodless categories." But his was too robust a mind to suppose that the limitation of our intellect could enable us to dispense with it and run loose with vague words about life, instinct, or *élan vital,* which can hardly cover the absence of definite ideas. The edifying certainties which begin where logic ends are but the opiates of weak minds. Intellectual virility shows itself in fearlessly facing the abysmal darkness that envelops us and in persistently applying logic to experience—which is the tantalizingly slow methed by which science extends the realm of human habitation. Painfully—I think too painfully—aware of the limitation of all intellectual construction, Bradley's clear and strong faith in metaphysics pulverizes its unimaginative critics who think that we can gain wisdom by blindly hoarding "facts."

The notes and terminal essays added to this edition indicate how implicit in this book are Bradley's later works. His *Appearance and Reality* towers higher as a brilliant intellectual achievement, and his *Essays on Truth and Reality* shines with a more mellow light. But as a work of substantial insight and of continued usefulness to workers in this field of human endeavor, this *Logic* excels. Yet it also best shows the defects of Bradley's noble qualities. Bradley's great strength, I have tried to indicate, lies in his holding fast to both poles of human thought, the immediacy of feeling and the unimaginable totality of all things which we call the world and which our intellect must strive to understand. But whether because his invalidism prevented him from closely following the actual work of science, or whether because he was temperamentally incapable of liberating himself from the modern literary preoccupation with strong feelings, which makes the work of thought seem pale and lifeless, the fact remains that Bradley did not do full justice to the task of science in building intellectual paths between the two terminals of thought. Too lightly does he dismiss science as valid and useful but incompetent to put us in contact with reality—thus helping to spread the superstition that science is but a practical device or useful fiction. If science gives us no light on reality, the latter must remain essentially unknowable and we have no way of telling how it is related to the world of nature and known experience. All that Bradley can in fact tell us about reality is that in some essentially unknowable way it includes everything. He has no satisfactory way of distinguishing between truth and error. To say as he does that all humanly attainable truths are unreal and that all errors are somehow partial truths, throws little light on the actual world and on the human struggle against error and illusion. Propositions like $2 + 2 = 4$ may not carry us very far in the apprehension of the total reality, but they are absolutely different from propositions like $2 + 2 = 5$. As creatures of sense and time, the absolute totality of the world is for us necessarily an unattainable limit. But the necessary effort after the unattainable which characterizes thought and all distinctively human effort, is made intelligible if we remember that we must actually have an ideal of the absolute sufficiently definite to recognize that our partial attainments fall short of it. It is the possession of this ideal which enables science to discriminate between the true and the false, and to evaluate the more or less true. In thus recognizing our eternal inability to attain an actual absolute we possess an ideal absolute. Is this distinction too finely drawn? It is at bottom the distinction between all doctrines which regard the human task as infinite, necessary, and intelligible though full of tragedy, and doctrines which flatter our frail vanity by trying to persuade us that some favorite creed, institution or panacea will forever withstand the ravages of time and mortal finitude.

2

John Dewey [2]

With that admirable self-restraint characteristic of the genuine scientist, Professor Dewey has restricted his life work to the seemingly narrow specialty—the study of how people think and how their thoughts become effective. His contributions to the field of education and to the method of ethical and political discussion, are applications and illustrations of his central theses. To his task Professor Dewey brings a marvelous power of seeing elusive mental events as they occur in all their fullness; and though he has not William James's genius for bringing forth burning words, his greater mastery of philosophical technique and his larger armory of dialectic weapons compel greater attention from philosophers, who, like other professionals, cannot admit the possibility of good music where there is no obvious virtuosity. But though written for a technical audience without any extraneous attraction to relieve the close-knitting of the argument, the book before us is not without interest to the thoughtful layman. There are many indications that its pragmatism may soon become the popular philosophy of our progressive democracy—very much as the refined and almost austere simplicity of Epicurus became the professed philosophy of the gilded youth of imperial Rome.

It may seem strange that a thinker of such laborious, almost painful regard for accuracy, so distrustful of vague and easy generalities, should become the patron saint of a multitude who

[2] A review of John Dewey, *Essays in Experimental Logic*, first appearing in *The New Republic*, vol. 8 (1916), p. 118.

deal in watchwords, to whom the mere use of the words *genetic,*
functional, experimental, dynamic, and the like is the sole condition of intellectual salvation. But on closer consideration this
need not surprise us. Professor Dewey's intense earnestness and
sensitiveness and his absorption in the thoughts of the "man in
the street," rather than in those of the philosophers, naturally
make his utterance a fit apology or justification for that characteristic American attitude, so emphatically and unreflectingly
expressed by Theodore Roosevelt—the worship of the practical,
the adoration of deed or act above thought or reflection. Professor Dewey himself, it is true, remains faithful to the noble
tradition of philosophy, and in these days of nationalistic romantic anti-rationalism, typified by Bergson, he is one of the
very few to insist on the high value of thought. But note, it is
the value, not the dignity, of thought that he emphasizes. Like
William James he has the puritanic distrust of esthetic categories. He has, to be sure, repeatedly protested against the per-
sistent misinterpretation that his pragmatism makes knowledge
merely a means to practical ends of the bread-and-butter type,
and at times he explicitly admits that the pragmatic "practical"
may include such things as logical symmetry and harmony as
ends in themselves. But the great burden of his analysis and the
bulk of his illustrations emphasize ideas of sensory-motor ad-
justment directed to utilitarian considerations. Knowledge is
exclusively a means to control the physical environment. The
ancient passion for glory in philosophy thus gives place to the
passion for service in the common weal. If I were not convinced
that philosophic labels are libels, and if my reverence for Professor Dewey were not so high, I would have called him a naturalistic Puritan.

Among philosophers as among scientists we may roughly distinguish two types that may be called the mathematical and the
naturalistic. The mathematicians excel in grasping some fruitful idea and elaborating it with such a perfection or finality of
form that humanity is compelled, through sheer admiration, to
strain the facts to make them fit these perfect forms. The natural-

ists, on the other hand, are more eager to observe the actual
facts in their naked natural state. They love accuracy more than
elegance. That philosophers can write with their eye on the object of their observation rather than on the symmetry of their
final system, careful readers of Aristotle and Kant know full well.
Nevertheless, the prevailing temper among philosophers has
been the mathematical one; for all the great men of science
whose achievements have stirred the human imagination, from
the days of Euclid and Archimedes down to Copernicus, Galileo,
and Newton, have been mathematicians. It was only in the middle of the nineteenth century, and most notably in the case of
Darwin, that men of the naturalistic type succeeded in impress-
ing humanity with results of the first magnitude. I have no doubt
that the great significance of James and Dewey in the history of
philosophy will be set down as consisting in the fact that they
were the first (except for the little-known anticipatory work of
the mathematicians Cournot and Peirce), to make the conscious
effort to build up the whole of philosophy by the Darwinian
method. At any rate, in my own experience, this has been the
successful clue to the understanding of Dewey's position. For
several years as a student of philosophy I tried in vain to master
his philosophic system. No sooner did I suppose that I had at
last understood it, than he would publish a paper to prove that
I didn't. It was only when I gave up the attempt to see the philosophic "system," and began to read his essays as one reads the
essays of Emerson, that I began to see that here was a genuine
new approach to the sorely tried and baffling problems of philosophy.

The naturalistic temper shows itself curiously in the external
form of his writings. He does not give us any systematic treatise.
His numerous essays are like the successive reports of a naturalist, constantly coming back to the same object, viewing it again
and again from new points of view, and perpetually correcting
his earlier impressions. Though I have the hardihood to think
Professor Dewey's philosophy seriously defective in its Hegelian
distrust of the abstract, in its overemphasis of biologic analogies

and in its underestimating of the purely logical or mathematical element of scientific truth, I think none of these defects inherent in the naturalistic method; they seem to me the fruit of an excess of zeal in a righteous cause and the inevitable tendency to deny through sheer emphasis the existence of the things outside the scope of our interests.

The basic idea of the whole pragmatic movement is that since thought has appeared in the course of man's struggle for existence, it must have a biologic function, that is, it must favor the survival of the organism. Having broken with the idea of design in nature, the idea that nature, like the prudent heroes of Samuel Smiles, never does anything purposeless or in vain, why should we swallow it in its biologic guise? The Darwinian ideas of adaptation, struggle and survival were doubtless useful in their day but they are being somewhat eclipsed in contemporary experimental biology. Certain it is that their indiscriminate application to the field of social and psychic life is not the prerequisite of scientific sanity, and on an empirical basis there is little evidence to connect the philosophical excellence of a mind like Plato's with the biologic survival of the species.

According to Professor Dewey all thinking begins because we get into trouble. In the beginning man dwells in a paradise of pure experience, knowing not the difference between truth and falsehood. But our paradise contains rival forces and their rivalry brings about a strain until through the labor of reflection man readjusts himself to the new situation. Doubtless this is largely true. So long as all goes well with Job he does not ask, Why do the righteous prosper? But I think there is also a great deal of thought that is the result of idle curiosity, or comes through sheer imitation. A certain idea like natural selection proves highly successful in one field and men at once try to apply it in all sorts of fields in which it has no appropriate place.

With all his radicalism Professor Dewey remains true to the Lockean tradition which regards the study of the constitution of knowledge as the true starting point in philosophy and thus tends to make the latter synonymous with mental science. Thus

Professor Dewey's experimental logic is a phenomenalistic psychology, an account of how men do think. To real logic, to an account of the general constitution of objects, of which the facts of psychology are only one species, Professor Dewey is certainly not friendly. Thus it becomes rather difficult to distinguish his philosophy from the anthropocentric view of the world which Schiller calls humanism. Indeed, the predominant emotional value of modern idealism and of pragmatism is the same: both are compensatory philosophies, reconciling man to scientific discoveries which have diminished his dignity as the center of creation. When the Copernican astronomy broke up the comfortable belief that all creation revolved about man's abode, idealism arose and said: Behold! your body may be a speck on a tiny particle of dust, but the whole character of the universe depends on consciousness. Now that Darwinism has broken down man's splendid isolation from the rest of the biologic world, the newer idealism and pragmatism try to use the very terms of Darwinism, evolution, adaptation, etc., to construct a picture of the world in which the *élan vital,* experience, and so on hold the central and dignified position. In vain does Professor Dewey insist that by experience he also means objects like chairs, which in some form pre-exist human knowledge. Words are stubborn things and do not readily submit to bearing unusual meanings. In spite of all warnings people will continue to take the word *experience* to denote some personal possession, an *Erlebnis.* Hence they will, also, fail to understand Professor Dewey's attitude to the belief which all scientific investigators share, namely, that there are more things in heaven and earth than are contained in our experience; or, in the language of Justice Holmes, that we are in the belly of the universe and not it in us.

The prevailing temper of American philosophy has been well expressed by one of our mid-western teachers when he said that philosophy should justify itself "not as an intellectual pastime, or as an emotional indulgence, nor yet as an escape from the unwelcome realities of our present existence but by its bearing on human weal and woe." This is a noble sentiment but not the embodiment of an accurate analysis of things. In the first place it ignores the fact that we live in a paradoxical world in which it happens to be true as a matter of historic fact that the men who have done most for human weal and woe have been precisely those who have pursued pure science as a pastime or as an escape from the monotony of empty life. Not a single advance in man's control over nature in modern times but is based on the work of men like Galileo, Newton or Lagrange, whose predominant passion was to find the simplest mathematical expression in which, they believed, the book of nature was written. We should never have had wireless electricity and the consequent saving—or destruction—of life, if Maxwell had devoted himself to the promotion of human welfare instead of speculating about the ether—which may not exist at all—and about the purely mathematical properties of electro-magnetic equations.

Still more important, however, is the recognition of the poverty of the conception of human weal and woe which does not include the pursuit of philosophy not only as a means but also as an end in itself. Too many current conceptions regard human welfare as consisting solely of instrumentalities by which life is prolonged or rendered physically more comfortable. But the things that make human life dignified and worth while are not the instrumentalities but certain things which are ends in themselves, the delights of companionship, the joy of creative activity, the vision of beauty, and not least the unique privilege of being for a brief space a spectator of the great drama of existence in which solar systems are born and destroyed—a drama in which our part as actors is of infinitesimal significance.

There are several passages in Professor Dewey's writings which may be construed as partial admissions of the foregoing contention. But these admissions do not determine the trend of his philosophy, which is dominated throughout by what I must regard as an unwise fear of otherworldliness. It is true that the glorification of the contemplative life has led, as in the case of the Greek or Russian Church, to a mysticism that is downright filthy. But it is not meet for philosophy because one extreme is vicious to jump to the opposite extreme, which may be no better.

The too ardent desire to make philosophy a means to improve the world, seems to me the source of the limitations of Professor Dewey's educational and political philosophy. I have no sympathy with the fatuity of the old classical education, and am heartily in favor of an education which will enable the great majority to have a better understanding and control of their actual environment. But so long as our world remains so far from our heart's desire, any philosophy of education which does not also enable one to build a haven into which he can for a time escape from the suffocating cruelties of every-day life, is needlessly cruel. Does not wisdom consist in apportioning time for work and time for play, time to live with others and time to live with one's self?

In politics the prime object of Professor Dewey's aversion, ideals divorced from actualities, would perhaps be best embodied in the impossible *a priori* program of the old Socialist Labor party, and I suppose the logical consequence of his views would be a practical program of reform that would progressively improve all the conditions of municipal, state and national life. But though the latter course is my own preference as a citizen, I am not sure that it is always the wisest course. Whenever I think of this question the pale face of a socialist tailor that I once knew comes to my mind. Possessed of remarkable intellectual and literary gifts, his life was wrecked by commonplace poverty and hard work. As I recall how his deep-set eyes would lighten up and his whole figure be transformed as he explained that by voting the Socialist ticket he was dealing the death-blow to the capitalist system and laying the sure foundation of the beatific co-operative commonwealth, I wonder whether a practical reform party which might have helped to increase his wages or reduce the number of hours, could so have lifted his life out of the sodden dreariness through which so many have to bear their burden

INDEX

Index

A CATALOGUE OF
SELECTED DOVER BOOKS
IN ALL FIELDS OF INTEREST

A CATALOGUE OF SELECTED DOVER
BOOKS IN ALL FIELDS OF INTEREST

RACKHAM'S COLOR ILLUSTRATIONS FOR WAGNER'S RING. Rackham's finest mature work—all 64 full-color watercolors in a faithful and lush interpretation of the *Ring*. Full-sized plates on coated stock of the paintings used by opera companies for authentic staging of Wagner. Captions aid in following complete Ring cycle. Introduction. 64 illustrations plus vignettes. 72pp. 8⅝ x 11¼. 23779-6 Pa. $6.00

CONTEMPORARY POLISH POSTERS IN FULL COLOR, edited by Joseph Czestochowski. 46 full-color examples of brilliant school of Polish graphic design, selected from world's first museum (near Warsaw) dedicated to poster art. Posters on circuses, films, plays, concerts all show cosmopolitan influences, free imagination. Introduction. 48pp. 9⅜ x 12¼. 23780-X Pa. $6.00

GRAPHIC WORKS OF EDVARD MUNCH, Edvard Munch. 90 haunting, evocative prints by first major Expressionist artist and one of the greatest graphic artists of his time: *The Scream, Anxiety, Death Chamber, The Kiss, Madonna,* etc. Introduction by Alfred Werner. 90pp. 9 x 12. 23765-6 Pa. $5.00

THE GOLDEN AGE OF THE POSTER, Hayward and Blanche Cirker. 70 extraordinary posters in full colors, from Maitres de l'Affiche, Mucha, Lautrec, Bradley, Cheret, Beardsley, many others. Total of 78pp. 9⅜ x 12¼. 22753-7 Pa. $5.95

THE NOTEBOOKS OF LEONARDO DA VINCI, edited by J. P. Richter. Extracts from manuscripts reveal great genius; on painting, sculpture, anatomy, sciences, geography, etc. Both Italian and English. 186 ms. pages reproduced, plus 500 additional drawings, including studies for *Last Supper*, Sforza monument, etc. 860pp. 7⅞ x 10¾. (Available in U.S. only) 22572-0, 22573-9 Pa., Two-vol. set $15.90

THE CODEX NUTTALL, as first edited by Zelia Nuttall. Only inexpensive edition, in full color, of a pre-Columbian Mexican (Mixtec) book. 88 color plates show kings, gods, heroes, temples, sacrifices. New explanatory, historical introduction by Arthur G. Miller. 96pp. 11⅜ x 8½. (Available in U.S. only) 23168-2 Pa. $7.95

UNE SEMAINE DE BONTÉ, A SURREALISTIC NOVEL IN COLLAGE, Max Ernst. Masterpiece created out of 19th-century periodical illustrations, explores worlds of terror and surprise. Some consider this Ernst's greatest work. 208pp. 8⅛ x 11. 23252-2 Pa. $6.00

DRAWINGS OF WILLIAM BLAKE, William Blake. 92 plates from Book of Job, *Divine Comedy, Paradise Lost,* visionary heads, mythological figures, Laocoon, etc. Selection, introduction, commentary by Sir Geoffrey Keynes. 178pp. 8⅛ x 11. 22303-5 Pa. $4.00

ENGRAVINGS OF HOGARTH, William Hogarth. 101 of Hogarth's greatest works: *Rake's Progress, Harlot's Progress, Illustrations for Hudibras, Before and After, Beer Street and Gin Lane,* many more. Full commentary. 256pp. 11 x 13¾. 22479-1 Pa. $12.95

DAUMIER: 120 GREAT LITHOGRAPHS, Honore Daumier. Wide-ranging collection of lithographs by the greatest caricaturist of the 19th century. Concentrates on eternally popular series on lawyers, on married life, on liberated women, etc. Selection, introduction, and notes on plates by Charles F. Ramus. Total of 158pp. 9⅜ x 12¼. 23512-2 Pa. $6.00

DRAWINGS OF MUCHA, Alphonse Maria Mucha. Work reveals drafts-man of highest caliber: studies for famous posters and paintings, render-ings for book illustrations and ads, etc. 70 works, 9 in color; including 6 items not drawings. Introduction. List of illustrations. 72pp. 9⅜ x 12¼. (Available in U.S. only) 23672-2 Pa. $4.00

GIOVANNI BATTISTA PIRANESI: DRAWINGS IN THE PIERPONT MORGAN LIBRARY, Giovanni Battista Piranesi. For first time ever all of Morgan Library's collection, world's largest. 167 illustrations of rare Piranesi drawings—archeological, architectural, decorative and visionary. Essay, detailed list of drawings, chronology, captions. Edited by Felice Stampfle. 144pp. 9⅜ x 12¼. 23714-1 Pa. $7.50

NEW YORK ETCHINGS (1905-1949), John Sloan. All of important American artist's N.Y. life etchings. 67 works include some of his best art; also lively historical record—Greenwich Village, tenement scenes. Edited by Sloan's widow. Introduction and captions. 79pp. 8⅜ x 11¼. 23651-X Pa. $4.00

CHINESE PAINTING AND CALLIGRAPHY: A PICTORIAL SURVEY, Wan-go Weng. 69 fine examples from John M. Crawford's matchless private collection: landscapes, birds, flowers, human figures, etc., plus calligraphy. Every basic form included: hanging scrolls, handscrolls, album leaves, fans, etc. 109 illustrations. Introduction. Captions. 192pp. 8⅞ x 11¾. 23707-9 Pa. $7.95

DRAWINGS OF REMBRANDT, edited by Seymour Slive. Updated Lipp-mann, Hofstede de Groot edition, with definitive scholarly apparatus. All portraits, biblical sketches, landscapes, nudes, Oriental figures, classical studies, together with selection of work by followers. 550 illustrations. Total of 630pp. 9⅛ x 12¼. 21485-0, 21486-9 Pa., Two-vol. set $15.00

THE DISASTERS OF WAR, Francisco Goya. 83 etchings record horrors of Napoleonic wars in Spain and war in general. Reprint of 1st edition, plus 3 additional plates. Introduction by Philip Hofer. 97pp. 9⅜ x 8¼. 21872-4 Pa. $4.00

THE EARLY WORK OF AUBREY BEARDSLEY, Aubrey Beardsley. 157 plates, 2 in color: *Manon Lescaut, Madame Bovary, Morte Darthur, Salome,* other. Introduction by H. Marillier. 182pp. 8⅛ x 11. 21816-3 Pa. $4.50

THE LATER WORK OF AUBREY BEARDSLEY, Aubrey Beardsley. Exotic masterpieces of full maturity: *Venus and Tannhauser, Lysistrata, Rape of the Lock, Volpone,* Savoy material, etc. 174 plates, 2 in color. 186pp. 8⅛ x 11. 21817-1 Pa. $5.95

THOMAS NAST'S CHRISTMAS DRAWINGS, Thomas Nast. Almost all Christmas drawings by creator of image of Santa Claus as we know it, and one of America's foremost illustrators and political cartoonists. 66 illustrations. 3 illustrations in color on covers. 96pp. 8⅜ x 11¼. 23660-9 Pa. $3.50

THE DORÉ ILLUSTRATIONS FOR DANTE'S DIVINE COMEDY, Gustave Doré. All 135 plates from Inferno, Purgatory, Paradise; fantastic tortures, infernal landscapes, celestial wonders. Each plate with appropriate (translated) verses. 141pp. 9 x 12. 23231-X Pa. $4.50

DORÉ'S ILLUSTRATIONS FOR RABELAIS, Gustave Doré. 252 striking illustrations of *Gargantua and Pantagruel* books by foremost 19th-century illustrator. Including 60 plates, 192 delightful smaller illustrations. 153pp. 9 x 12. 23656-0 Pa. $5.00

LONDON: A PILGRIMAGE, Gustave Doré, Blanchard Jerrold. Squalor, riches, misery, beauty of mid-Victorian metropolis; 55 wonderful plates, 125 other illustrations, full social, cultural text by Jerrold. 191pp. of text. 9⅜ x 12¼. 22306-X Pa. $7.00

THE RIME OF THE ANCIENT MARINER, Gustave Doré, S. T. Coleridge. Dore's finest work, 34 plates capture moods, subtleties of poem. Full text. Introduction by Millicent Rose. 77pp. 9¼ x 12. 22305-1 Pa. $3.50

THE DORE BIBLE ILLUSTRATIONS, Gustave Doré. All wonderful, detailed plates: Adam and Eve, Flood, Babylon, Life of Jesus, etc. Brief King James text with each plate. Introduction by Millicent Rose. 241 plates. 241pp. 9 x 12. 23004-X Pa. $6.00

THE COMPLETE ENGRAVINGS, ETCHINGS AND DRYPOINTS OF ALBRECHT DURER. "Knight, Death and Devil"; "Melencolia," and more—all Dürer's known works in all three media, including 6 works formerly attributed to him. 120 plates. 235pp. 8⅜ x 11¼. 22851-7 Pa. $6.50

MECHANICK EXERCISES ON THE WHOLE ART OF PRINTING, Joseph Moxon. First complete book (1683-4) ever written about typography, a compendium of everything known about printing at the latter part of 17th century. Reprint of 2nd (1962) Oxford Univ. Press edition. 74 illustrations. Total of 550pp. 6⅛ x 9¼. 23617-X Pa. $7.95

THE COMPLETE WOODCUTS OF ALBRECHT DURER, edited by Dr. W. Kurth. 346 in all: "Old Testament," "St. Jerome," "Passion," "Life of Virgin," Apocalypse," many others. Introduction by Campbell Dodgson. 285pp. 8½ x 12¼. 21097-9 Pa. $7.50

DRAWINGS OF ALBRECHT DURER, edited by Heinrich Wolfflin. 81 plates show development from youth to full style. Many favorites; many new. Introduction by Alfred Werner. 96pp. 8⅛ x 11. 22352-3 Pa. $5.00

THE HUMAN FIGURE, Albrecht Dürer. Experiments in various techniques—stereometric, progressive proportional, and others. Also life studies that rank among finest ever done. Complete reprinting of *Dresden Sketchbook*. 170 plates. 355pp. 8⅜ x 11¼. 21042-1 Pa. $7.95

OF THE JUST SHAPING OF LETTERS, Albrecht Dürer. Renaissance artist explains design of Roman majuscules by geometry, also Gothic lower and capitals. Grolier Club edition. 43pp. 7⅞ x 10¾ 21306-4 Pa. $3.00

TEN BOOKS ON ARCHITECTURE, Vitruvius. The most important book ever written on architecture. Early Roman aesthetics, technology, classical orders, site selection, all other aspects. Stands behind everything since. Morgan translation. 331pp. 5⅜ x 8½. 20645-9 Pa. $4.50

THE FOUR BOOKS OF ARCHITECTURE, Andrea Palladio. 16th-century classic responsible for Palladian movement and style. Covers classical architectural remains, Renaissance revivals, classical orders, etc. 1738 Ware English edition. Introduction by A. Placzek. 216 plates. 110pp. of text. 9½ x 12¾. 21308-0 Pa. $10.00

HORIZONS, Norman Bel Geddes. Great industrialist stage designer, "father of streamlining," on application of aesthetics to transportation, amusement, architecture, etc. 1932 prophetic account; function, theory, specific projects. 222 illustrations. 312pp. 7⅞ x 10¾. 23514-9 Pa. $6.95

FRANK LLOYD WRIGHT'S FALLINGWATER, Donald Hoffmann. Full, illustrated story of conception and building of Wright's masterwork at Bear Run, Pa. 100 photographs of site, construction, and details of completed structure. 112pp. 9¼ x 10. 23671-4 Pa. $5.50

THE ELEMENTS OF DRAWING, John Ruskin. Timeless classic by great Viltorian; starts with basic ideas, works through more difficult. Many practical exercises. 48 illustrations. Introduction by Lawrence Campbell. 228pp. 5⅜ x 8½. 22730-8 Pa. $3.75

GIST OF ART, John Sloan. Greatest modern American teacher, Art Students League, offers innumerable hints, instructions, guided comments to help you in painting. Not a formal course. 46 illustrations. Introduction by Helen Sloan. 200pp. 5⅜ x 8½. 23435-5 Pa. $4.00

THE ANATOMY OF THE HORSE, George Stubbs. Often considered the great masterpiece of animal anatomy. Full reproduction of 1766 edition, plus prospectus; original text and modernized text. 36 plates. Introduction by Eleanor Garvey. 121pp. 11 x 14¾.   23402-9 Pa. $6.00

BRIDGMAN'S LIFE DRAWING, George B. Bridgman. More than 500 illustrative drawings and text teach you to abstract the body into its major masses, use light and shade, proportion; as well as specific areas of anatomy, of which Bridgman is master. 192pp. 6½ x 9¼. (Available in U.S. only) 22710-3 Pa. $3.50

ART NOUVEAU DESIGNS IN COLOR, Alphonse Mucha, Maurice Verneuil, Georges Auriol. Full-color reproduction of *Combinaisons ornementales* (c. 1900) by Art Nouveau masters. Floral, animal, geometric, interlacings, swashes—borders, frames, spots—all incredibly beautiful. 60 plates, hundreds of designs. 9⅜ x 8-1/16.   22885-1 Pa. $4.00

FULL-COLOR FLORAL DESIGNS IN THE ART NOUVEAU STYLE, E. A. Seguy. 166 motifs, on 40 plates, from *Les fleurs et leurs applications decoratives* (1902): borders, circular designs, repeats, allovers, "spots." All in authentic Art Nouveau colors. 48pp. 9⅜ x 12¼.
23439-8 Pa. $5.00

A DIDEROT PICTORIAL ENCYCLOPEDIA OF TRADES AND IN-DUSTRY, edited by Charles C. Gillispie. 485 most interesting plates from the great French Encyclopedia of the 18th century show hundreds of working figures, artifacts, process, land and cityscapes; glassmaking, paper-making, metal extraction, construction, weaving, making furniture, clothing, wigs, dozens of other activities. Plates fully explained. 920pp. 9 x 12.
22284-5, 22285-3 Clothbd., Two-vol. set $40.00

HANDBOOK OF EARLY ADVERTISING ART, Clarence P. Hornung. Largest collection of copyright-free early and antique advertising art ever compiled. Over 6,000 illustrations, from Franklin's time to the 1890's for special effects, novelty. Valuable source, almost inexhaustible.
Pictorial Volume. Agriculture, the zodiac, animals, autos, birds, Christmas, fire engines, flowers, trees, musical instruments, ships, games and sports, much more. Arranged by subject matter and use. 237 plates. 288pp. 9 x 12.
20122-8 Clothbd. $14..50

Typographical Volume. Roman and Gothic faces ranging from 10 point to 300 point, "Barnum," German and Old English faces, script, logotypes, scrolls and flourishes, 1115 ornamental initials, 67 complete alphabets, more. 310 plates. 320pp. 9 x 12.   20123-6 Clothbd. $15.00

CALLIGRAPHY (CALLIGRAPHIA LATINA), J. G. Schwandner. High point of 18th-century ornamental calligraphy. Very ornate initials, scrolls, borders, cherubs, birds, lettered examples. 172pp. 9 x 13.
20475-8 Pa. $7.00

ART FORMS IN NATURE, Ernst Haeckel. Multitude of strangely beautiful natural forms: Radiolaria, Foraminifera, jellyfishes, fungi, turtles, bats, etc. All 100 plates of the 19th-century evolutionist's *Kunstformen der Natur* (1904). 100pp. 9⅜ x 12¼. 22987-4 Pa. $5.00

CHILDREN: A PICTORIAL ARCHIVE FROM NINETEENTH-CENTURY SOURCES, edited by Carol Belanger Grafton. 242 rare, copyright-free wood engravings for artists and designers. Widest such selection available. All illustrations in line. 119pp. 8⅜ x 11¼.
23694-3 Pa. $4.00

WOMEN: A PICTORIAL ARCHIVE FROM NINETEENTH-CENTURY SOURCES, edited by Jim Harter. 391 copyright-free wood engravings for artists and designers selected from rare periodicals. Most extensive such collection available. All illustrations in line. 128pp. 9 x 12.
23703-6 Pa. $4.50

ARABIC ART IN COLOR, Prisse d'Avennes. From the greatest ornamentalists of all time—50 plates in color, rarely seen outside the Near East, rich in suggestion and stimulus. Includes 4 plates on covers. 46pp. 9⅜ x 12¼. 23658-7 Pa. $6.00

AUTHENTIC ALGERIAN CARPET DESIGNS AND MOTIFS, edited by June Beveridge. Algerian carpets are world famous. Dozens of geometrical motifs are charted on grids, color-coded, for weavers, needleworkers, craftsmen, designers. 53 illustrations plus 4 in color. 48pp. 8¼ x 11. (Available in U.S. only) 23650-1 Pa. $1.75

DICTIONARY OF AMERICAN PORTRAITS, edited by Hayward and Blanche Cirker. 4000 important Americans, earliest times to 1905, mostly in clear line. Politicians, writers, soldiers, scientists, inventors, industrialists, Indians, Blacks, women, outlaws, etc. Identificatory information. 756pp. 9¼ x 12¾. 21823-6 Clothbd. $40.00

HOW THE OTHER HALF LIVES, Jacob A. Riis. Journalistic record of filth, degradation, upward drive in New York immigrant slums, shops, around 1900. New edition includes 100 original Riis photos, monuments of early photography. 233pp. 10 x 7⅞. 22012-5 Pa. $7.00

NEW YORK IN THE THIRTIES, Berenice Abbott. Noted photographer's fascinating study of city shows new buildings that have become famous and old sights that have disappeared forever. Insightful commentary. 97 photographs. 97pp. 11⅜ x 10. 22967-X Pa. $5.00

MEN AT WORK, Lewis W. Hine. Famous photographic studies of construction workers, railroad men, factory workers and coal miners. New supplement of 18 photos on Empire State building construction. New introduction by Jonathan L. Doherty. Total of 69 photos. 63pp. 8 x 10¾.
23475-4 Pa. $3.00

THE DEPRESSION YEARS AS PHOTOGRAPHED BY ARTHUR ROTH-STEIN, Arthur Rothstein. First collection devoted entirely to the work of outstanding 1930s photographer: famous dust storm photo, ragged children, unemployed, etc. 120 photographs. Captions. 119pp. 9¼ x 10¾.
23590-4 Pa. $5.00

CAMERA WORK: A PICTORIAL GUIDE, Alfred Stieglitz. All 559 illustrations and plates from the most important periodical in the history of art photography, Camera Work (1903-17). Presented four to a page, reduced in size but still clear, in strict chronological order, with complete captions. Three indexes. Glossary. Bibliography. 176pp. 8⅜ x 11¼.
23591-2 Pa. $6.95

ALVIN LANGDON COBURN, PHOTOGRAPHER, Alvin L. Coburn. Revealing autobiography by one of greatest photographers of 20th century gives insider's version of Photo-Secession, plus comments on his own work. 77 photographs by Coburn. Edited by Helmut and Alison Gernsheim. 160pp. 8⅛ x 11.
23685-4 Pa. $6.00

NEW YORK IN THE FORTIES, Andreas Feininger. 162 brilliant photographs by the well-known photographer, formerly with Life magazine, show commuters, shoppers, Times Square at night, Harlem nightclub, Lower East Side, etc. Introduction and full captions by John von Hartz. 181pp. 9¼ x 10¾.
23585-8 Pa. $6.95

GREAT NEWS PHOTOS AND THE STORIES BEHIND THEM, John Faber. Dramatic volume of 140 great news photos, 1855 through 1976, and revealing stories behind them, with both historical and technical information. Hindenburg disaster, shooting of Oswald, nomination of Jimmy Carter, etc. 160pp. 8¼ x 11.
23667-6 Pa. $5.00

THE ART OF THE CINEMATOGRAPHER, Leonard Maltin. Survey of American cinematography history and anecdotal interviews with 5 masters—Arthur Miller, Hal Mohr, Hal Rosson, Lucien Ballard, and Conrad Hall. Very large selection of behind-the-scenes production photos. 105 photographs. Filmographies. Index. Originally Behind the Camera. 144pp. 8¼ x 11.
23686-2 Pa. $5.00

DESIGNS FOR THE THREE-CORNERED HAT (LE TRICORNE), Pablo Picasso. 32 fabulously rare drawings—including 31 color illustrations of costumes and accessories—for 1919 production of famous ballet. Edited by Parmenia Migel, who has written new introduction. 48pp. 9⅜ x 12¼. (Available in U.S. only)
23709-5 Pa. $5.00

NOTES OF A FILM DIRECTOR, Sergei Eisenstein. Greatest Russian filmmaker explains montage, making of Alexander Nevsky, aesthetics; comments on self, associates, great rivals (Chaplin), similar material. 78 illustrations. 240pp. 5⅜ x 8½.
22392-2 Pa. $4.50

HOLLYWOOD GLAMOUR PORTRAITS, edited by John Kobal. 145 photos capture the stars from 1926-49, the high point in portrait photography. Gable, Harlow, Bogart, Bacall, Hedy Lamarr, Marlene Dietrich, Robert Montgomery, Marlon Brando, Veronica Lake; 94 stars in all. Full background on photographers, technical aspects, much more. Total of 160pp. 8⅜ x 11¼.   23352-9 Pa. $6.00

THE NEW YORK STAGE: FAMOUS PRODUCTIONS IN PHOTO-GRAPHS, edited by Stanley Appelbaum. 148 photographs from Museum of City of New York show 142 plays, 1883-1939. *Peter Pan, The Front Page, Dead End, Our Town,* O'Neill, hundreds of actors and actresses, etc. Full indexes. 154pp. 9½ x 10.   23241-7 Pa. $6.00

DIALOGUES CONCERNING TWO NEW SCIENCES, Galileo Galilei. Encompassing 30 years of experiment and thought, these dialogues deal with geometric demonstrations of fracture of solid bodies, cohesion, leverage, speed of light and sound, pendulums, falling bodies, accelerated motion, etc. 300pp. 5⅜ x 8½.   60099-8 Pa. $4.00

THE GREAT OPERA STARS IN HISTORIC PHOTOGRAPHS, edited by James Camner. 343 portraits from the 1850s to the 1940s: Tamburini, Mario, Caliapin, Jeritza, Melchior, Melba, Patti, Pinza, Schipa, Caruso, Farrar, Steber, Gobbi, and many more—270 performers in all. Index. 199pp. 8⅜ x 11¼.   23575-0 Pa. $7.50

J. S. BACH, Albert Schweitzer. Great full-length study of Bach, life, background to music, music, by foremost modern scholar. Ernest Newman translation. 650 musical examples. Total of 928pp. 5⅜ x 8½. (Available in U.S. only)   21631-4, 21632-2 Pa., Two-vol. set $11.00

COMPLETE PIANO SONATAS, Ludwig van Beethoven. All sonatas in the fine Schenker edition, with fingering, analytical material. One of best modern editions. Total of 615pp. 9 x 12. (Available in U.S. only)
                              23134-8, 23135-6 Pa., Two-vol. set $15.50

KEYBOARD MUSIC, J. S. Bach. Bach-Gesellschaft edition. For harpsichord, piano, other keyboard instruments. English Suites, French Suites, Six Partitas, Goldberg Variations, Two-Part Inventions, Three-Part Sinfonias. 312pp. 8⅛ x 11. (Available in U.S. only)   22360-4 Pa. $6.95

FOUR SYMPHONIES IN FULL SCORE, Franz Schubert. Schubert's four most popular symphonies: No. 4 in C Minor ("Tragic"); No. 5 in B-flat Major; No. 8 in B Minor ("Unfinished"); No. 9 in C Major ("Great"). Breitkopf & Hartel edition. Study score. 261pp. 9⅜ x 12¼.
                                                       23681-1 Pa. $6.50

THE AUTHENTIC GILBERT & SULLIVAN SONGBOOK, W. S. Gilbert, A. S. Sullivan. Largest selection available; 92 songs, uncut, original keys, in piano rendering approved by Sullivan. Favorites and lesser-known fine numbers. Edited with plot synopses by James Spero. 3 illustrations. 399pp. 9 x 12.   23482-7 Pa. $9.95

PRINCIPLES OF ORCHESTRATION, Nikolay Rimsky-Korsakov. Great classical orchestrator provides fundamentals of tonal resonance, progression of parts, voice and orchestra, tutti effects, much else in major document. 330pp. of musical excerpts. 489pp. 6½ x 9¼.   21266-1 Pa. $7.50

TRISTAN UND ISOLDE, Richard Wagner. Full orchestral score with complete instrumentation. Do not confuse with piano reduction. Commentary by Felix Mottl, great Wagnerian conductor and scholar. Study score. 655pp. 8⅛ x 11.   22915-7 Pa. $13.95

REQUIEM IN FULL SCORE, Giuseppe Verdi. Immensely popular with choral groups and music lovers. Republication of edition published by C. F. Peters, Leipzig, n. d. German frontmaker in English translation. Glossary. Text in Latin. Study score. 204pp. 9⅜ x 12¼.
23682-X Pa. $6.00

COMPLETE CHAMBER MUSIC FOR STRINGS, Felix Mendelssohn. All of Mendelssohn's chamber music: Octet, 2 Quintets, 6 Quartets, and Four Pieces for String Quartet. (Nothing with piano is included). Complete works edition (1874-7). Study score. 283 pp. 9⅜ x 12¼.
23679-X Pa. $7.50

POPULAR SONGS OF NINETEENTH-CENTURY AMERICA, edited by Richard Jackson. 64 most important songs: "Old Oaken Bucket," "Arkansas Traveler," "Yellow Rose of Texas," etc. Authentic original sheet music, full introduction and commentaries. 290pp. 9 x 12.   23270-0 Pa. $7.95

COLLECTED PIANO WORKS, Scott Joplin. Edited by Vera Brodsky Lawrence. Practically all of Joplin's piano works—rags, two-steps, marches, waltzes, etc., 51 works in all. Extensive introduction by Rudi Blesh. Total of 345pp. 9 x 12.   23106-2 Pa. $14.95

BASIC PRINCIPLES OF CLASSICAL BALLET, Agrippina Vaganova. Great Russian theoretician, teacher explains methods for teaching classical ballet; incorporates best from French, Italian, Russian schools. 118 illustrations. 175pp. 5⅜ x 8½.   22036-2 Pa. $2.50

CHINESE CHARACTERS, L. Wieger. Rich analysis of 2300 characters according to traditional systems into primitives. Historical-semantic analysis to phonetics (Classical Mandarin) and radicals. 820pp. 6⅛ x 9¼.
21321-8 Pa. $10.00

EGYPTIAN LANGUAGE: EASY LESSONS IN EGYPTIAN HIERO-GLYPHICS, E. A. Wallis Budge. Foremost Egyptologist offers Egyptian grammar, explanation of hieroglyphics, many reading texts, dictionary of symbols. 246pp. 5 x 7½. (Available in U.S. only)
21394-3 Clothbd. $7.50

AN ETYMOLOGICAL DICTIONARY OF MODERN ENGLISH, Ernest Weekley. Richest, fullest work, by foremost British lexicographer. Detailed word histories. Inexhaustible. Do not confuse this with Concise Etymological Dictionary, which is abridged. Total of 856pp. 6½ x 9¼.
21873-2, 21874-0 Pa., Two-vol. set $12.00

A MAYA GRAMMAR, Alfred M. Tozzer. Practical, useful English-language grammar by the Harvard anthropologist who was one of the three greatest American scholars in the area of Maya culture. Phonetics, grammatical processes, syntax, more. 301pp. 5⅜ x 8½.   23465-7 Pa. $4.00

THE JOURNAL OF HENRY D. THOREAU, edited by Bradford Torrey, F. H. Allen. Complete reprinting of 14 volumes, 1837-61, over two million words; the sourcebooks for *Walden*, etc. Definitive. All original sketches, plus 75 photographs. Introduction by Walter Harding. Total of 1804pp. 8½ x 12¼.   20312-3, 20313-1 Clothbd., Two-vol. set $70.00

CLASSIC GHOST STORIES, Charles Dickens and others. 18 wonderful stories you've wanted to reread: "The Monkey's Paw," "The House and the Brain," "The Upper Berth," "The Signalman," "Dracula's Guest," "The Tapestried Chamber," etc. Dickens, Scott, Mary Shelley, Stoker, etc. 330pp. 5⅜ x 8½.   20735-8 Pa. $4.50

SEVEN SCIENCE FICTION NOVELS, H. G. Wells. Full novels. *First Men in the Moon, Island of Dr. Moreau, War of the Worlds, Food of the Gods, Invisible Man, Time Machine, In the Days of the Comet.* A basic science-fiction library. 1015pp. 5⅜ x 8½. (Available in U.S. only)
20264-X Clothbd. $8.95

ARMADALE, Wilkie Collins. Third great mystery novel by the author of *The Woman in White* and *The Moonstone.* Ingeniously plotted narrative shows an exceptional command of character, incident and mood. Original magazine version with 40 illustrations. 597pp. 5⅜ x 8½.
23429-0 Pa. $6.00

MASTERS OF MYSTERY, H. Douglas Thomson. The first book in English (1931) devoted to history and aesthetics of detective story. Poe, Doyle, LeFanu, Dickens, many others, up to 1930. New introduction and notes by E. F. Bleiler. 288pp. 5⅜ x 8½. (Available in U.S. only)
23606-4 Pa. $4.00

FLATLAND, E. A. Abbott. Science-fiction classic explores life of 2-D being in 3-D world. Read also as introduction to thought about hyperspace. Introduction by Banesh Hoffmann. 16 illustrations. 103pp. 5⅜ x 8½.
20001-9 Pa. $2.00

THREE SUPERNATURAL NOVELS OF THE VICTORIAN PERIOD, edited, with an introduction, by E. F. Bleiler. Reprinted complete and unabridged, three great classics of the supernatural: *The Haunted Hotel* by Wilkie Collins, *The Haunted House at Latchford* by Mrs. J. H. Riddell, and *The Lost Stradivarius* by J. Meade Falkner. 325pp. 5⅜ x 8½.
22571-2 Pa. $4.00

AYESHA: THE RETURN OF "SHE," H. Rider Haggard. Virtuoso sequel featuring the great mythic creation, Ayesha, in an adventure that is fully as good as the first book, *She.* Original magazine version, with 47 original illustrations by Maurice Greiffenhagen. 189pp. 6½ x 9¼.
23649-8 Pa. $3.50

UNCLE SILAS, J. Sheridan LeFanu. Victorian Gothic mystery novel, considered by many best of period, even better than Collins or Dickens. Wonderful psychological terror. Introduction by Frederick Shroyer. 436pp. 5⅜ x 8½.   21715-9 Pa. $6.00

JURGEN, James Branch Cabell. The great erotic fantasy of the 1920's that delighted thousands, shocked thousands more. Full final text, Lane edition with 13 plates by Frank Pape. 346pp. 5⅜ x 8½.
                                                                23507-6 Pa. $4.50

THE CLAVERINGS, Anthony Trollope. Major novel, chronicling aspects of British Victorian society, personalities. Reprint of Cornhill serialization, 16 plates by M. Edwards; first reprint of full text. Introduction by Norman Donaldson. 412pp. 5⅜ x 8½.   23464-9 Pa. $5.00

KEPT IN THE DARK, Anthony Trollope. Unusual short novel about Victorian morality and abnormal psychology by the great English author. Probably the first American publication. Frontispiece by Sir John Millais. 92pp. 6½ x 9¼.   23609-9 Pa. $2.50

RALPH THE HEIR, Anthony Trollope. Forgotten tale of illegitimacy, inheritance. Master novel of Trollope's later years. Victorian country estates, clubs, Parliament, fox hunting, world of fully realized characters. Reprint of 1871 edition. 12 illustrations by F. A. Faser. 434pp. of text. 5⅜ x 8½.   23642-0 Pa. $5.00

YEKL and THE IMPORTED BRIDEGROOM AND OTHER STORIES OF THE NEW YORK GHETTO, Abraham Cahan. Film *Hester Street* based on *Yekl* (1896). Novel, other stories among first about Jewish immigrants of N.Y.'s East Side. Highly praised by W. D. Howells—Cahan "a new star of realism." New introduction by Bernard G. Richards. 240pp. 5⅜ x 8½.   22427-9 Pa. $3.50

THE HIGH PLACE, James Branch Cabell. Great fantasy writer's enchanting comedy of disenchantment set in 18th-century France. Considered by some critics to be even better than his famous *Jurgen*. 10 illustrations and numerous vignettes by noted fantasy artist Frank C. Pape. 320pp. 5⅜ x 8½.   23670-6 Pa. $4.00

ALICE'S ADVENTURES UNDER GROUND, Lewis Carroll. Facsimile of ms. Carroll gave Alice Liddell in 1864. Different in many ways from final Alice. Handlettered, illustrated by Carroll. Introduction by Martin Gardner. 128pp. 5⅜ x 8½.   21482-6 Pa. $2.50

FAVORITE ANDREW LANG FAIRY TALE BOOKS IN MANY COLORS, Andrew Lang. The four Lang favorites in a boxed set—the complete *Red, Green, Yellow* and *Blue* Fairy Books. 164 stories; 439 illustrations by Lancelot Speed, Henry Ford and G. P. Jacomb Hood. Total of about 1500pp. 5⅜ x 8½.   23407-X Boxed set, Pa. $15.95

HOUSEHOLD STORIES BY THE BROTHERS GRIMM. All the great Grimm stories: "Rumpelstiltskin," "Snow White," "Hansel and Gretel," etc., with 114 illustrations by Walter Crane. 269pp. 5⅜ x 8½.
21080-4 Pa. $3.50

SLEEPING BEAUTY, illustrated by Arthur Rackham. Perhaps the fullest, most delightful version ever, told by C. S. Evans. Rackham's best work. 49 illustrations. 110pp. 7⅞ x 10¾.
22756-1 Pa. $2.50

AMERICAN FAIRY TALES, L. Frank Baum. Young cowboy lassoes Father Time; dummy in Mr. Floman's department store window comes to life; and 10 other fairy tales. 41 illustrations by N. P. Hall, Harry Kennedy, Ike Morgan, and Ralph Gardner. 209pp. 5⅜ x 8½.
23643-9 Pa. $3.00

THE WONDERFUL WIZARD OF OZ, L. Frank Baum. Facsimile in full color of America's finest children's classic. Introduction by Martin Gardner. 143 illustrations by W. W. Denslow. 267pp. 5⅜ x 8½.
20691-2 Pa. $3.50

THE TALE OF PETER RABBIT, Beatrix Potter. The inimitable Peter's terrifying adventure in Mr. McGregor's garden, with all 27 wonderful, full-color Potter illustrations. 55pp. 4¼ x 5½. (Available in U.S. only)
22827-4 Pa. $1.25

THE STORY OF KING ARTHUR AND HIS KNIGHTS, Howard Pyle. Finest children's version of life of King Arthur. 48 illustrations by Pyle. 131pp. 6⅛ x 9¼.
21445-1 Pa. $4.95

CARUSO'S CARICATURES, Enrico Caruso. Great tenor's remarkable caricatures of self, fellow musicians, composers, others. Toscanini, Puccini, Farrar, etc. Impish, cutting, insightful. 473 illustrations. Preface by M. Sisca. 217pp. 8⅜ x 11¼.
23528-9 Pa. $6.95

PERSONAL NARRATIVE OF A PILGRIMAGE TO ALMADINAH AND MECCAH, Richard Burton. Great travel classic by remarkably colorful personality. Burton, disguised as a Moroccan, visited sacred shrines of Islam, narrowly escaping death. Wonderful observations of Islamic life, customs, personalities. 47 illustrations. Total of 959pp. 5⅜ x 8½.
21217-3, 21218-1 Pa., Two-vol. set $12.00

INCIDENTS OF TRAVEL IN YUCATAN, John L. Stephens. Classic (1843) exploration of jungles of Yucatan, looking for evidences of Maya civilization. Travel adventures, Mexican and Indian culture, etc. Total of 669pp. 5⅜ x 8½.
20926-1, 20927-X Pa., Two-vol. set $7.90

AMERICAN LITERARY AUTOGRAPHS FROM WASHINGTON IRVING TO HENRY JAMES, Herbert Cahoon, et al. Letters, poems, manuscripts of Hawthorne, Thoreau, Twain, Alcott, Whitman, 67 other prominent American authors. Reproductions, full transcripts and commentary. Plus checklist of all American Literary Autographs in The Pierpont Morgan Library. Printed on exceptionally high-quality paper. 136 illustrations. 212pp. 9⅛ x 12¼.
23548-3 Pa. $12.50

AN AUTOBIOGRAPHY, Margaret Sanger. Exciting personal account of hard-fought battle for woman's right to birth control, against prejudice, church, law. Foremost feminist document. 504pp. 5⅜ x 8½.
20470-7 Pa. $5.50

MY BONDAGE AND MY FREEDOM, Frederick Douglass. Born as a slave, Douglass became outspoken force in antislavery movement. The best of Douglass's autobiographies. Graphic description of slave life. Introduction by P. Foner. 464pp. 5⅜ x 8½.
22457-0 Pa. $5.50

LIVING MY LIFE, Emma Goldman. Candid, no holds barred account by foremost American anarchist: her own life, anarchist movement, famous contemporaries, ideas and their impact. Struggles and confrontations in America, plus deportation to U.S.S.R. Shocking inside account of persecution of anarchists under Lenin. 13 plates. Total of 944pp. 5⅜ x 8½.
22543-7, 22544-5 Pa., Two-vol. set $12.00

LETTERS AND NOTES ON THE MANNERS, CUSTOMS AND CONDITIONS OF THE NORTH AMERICAN INDIANS, George Catlin. Classic account of life among Plains Indians: ceremonies, hunt, warfare, etc. Dover edition reproduces for first time all original paintings. 312 plates. 572pp. of text. 6⅛ x 9¼.
22118-0, 22119-9 Pa.. Two-vol. set $12.00

THE MAYA AND THEIR NEIGHBORS, edited by Clarence L. Hay, others. Synoptic view of Maya civilization in broadest sense, together with Northern, Southern neighbors. Integrates much background, valuable detail not elsewhere. Prepared by greatest scholars: Kroeber, Morley, Thompson, Spinden, Vaillant, many others. Sometimes called Tozzer Memorial Volume. 60 illustrations, linguistic map. 634pp. 5⅜ x 8½.
23510-6 Pa. $10.00

HANDBOOK OF THE INDIANS OF CALIFORNIA, A. L. Kroeber. Foremost American anthropologist offers complete ethnographic study of each group. Monumental classic. 459 illustrations, maps. 995pp. 5⅜ x 8½.
23368-5 Pa. $13.00

SHAKTI AND SHAKTA, Arthur Avalon. First book to give clear, cohesive analysis of Shakta doctrine, Shakta ritual and Kundalini Shakti (yoga). Important work by one of world's foremost students of Shaktic and Tantric thought. 732pp. 5⅜ x 8½. (Available in U.S. only)
23645-5 Pa. $7.95

AN INTRODUCTION TO THE STUDY OF THE MAYA HIEROGLYPHS, Syvanus Griswold Morley. Classic study by one of the truly great figures in hieroglyph research. Still the best introduction for the student for reading Maya hieroglyphs. New introduction by J. Eric S. Thompson. 117 illustrations. 284pp. 5⅜ x 8½.
23108-9 Pa. $4.00

A STUDY OF MAYA ART, Herbert J. Spinden. Landmark classic interprets Maya symbolism, estimates styles, covers ceramics, architecture, murals, stone carvings as artforms. Still a basic book in area. New introduction by J. Eric Thompson. Over 750 illustrations. 341pp. 8⅜ x 11¼.
21235-1 Pa. $6.95

GEOMETRY, RELATIVITY AND THE FOURTH DIMENSION, Rudolf Rucker. Exposition of fourth dimension, means of visualization, concepts of relativity as Flatland characters continue adventures. Popular, easily followed yet accurate, profound. 141 illustrations. 133pp. 5⅜ x 8½.
23400-2 Pa. $2.75

THE ORIGIN OF LIFE, A. I. Oparin. Modern classic in biochemistry, the first rigorous examination of possible evolution of life from nitrocarbon compounds. Non-technical, easily followed. Total of 295pp. 5⅜ x 8½.
60213-3 Pa. $4.00

PLANETS, STARS AND GALAXIES, A. E. Fanning. Comprehensive introductory survey: the sun, solar system, stars, galaxies, universe, cosmology; quasars, radio stars, etc. 24pp. of photographs. 189pp. 5⅜ x 8½. (Available in U.S. only)
21680-2 Pa. $3.75

THE THIRTEEN BOOKS OF EUCLID'S ELEMENTS, translated with introduction and commentary by Sir Thomas L. Heath. Definitive edition. Textual and linguistic notes, mathematical analysis, 2500 years of critical commentary. Do not confuse with abridged school editions. Total of 1414pp. 5⅜ x 8½. 60088-2, 60089-0, 60090-4 Pa., Three-vol. set $18.50

Prices subject to change without notice.

Available at your book dealer or write for free catalogue to Dept. GI, Dover Publications, Inc., 180 Varick St., N.Y., N.Y. 10014. Dover publishes more than 175 books each year on science, elementary and advanced mathematics, biology, music, art, literary history, social sciences and other areas.